ROLLING THUNDER

Stomping Out Indifference

By

Joyce Newell Sundheim

© 2018 Joyce Kassanonkwas Newell Sundheim - All rights reserved. Unauthorized use and/or duplication of any part of this material without express and written permission from the author is strictly prohibited. The moral right of Joyce Kassanonkwas Newell Sundheim (the author) has been asserted.

William Benjamin Newell (Taiowahronhagai)
and
Celina Canadian Newell (Kahwahnanorrah)

A Seneca Praise

Oh Great Mystery, we awake

To another sun

Grateful for the gifts bestowed

Granted one by one-

Grateful for the greatest gift,

The precious breath of life;

Grateful for abilities

That guides us day and night.

As we walk our chosen paths

Of lessons we must learn-

Spiritual peace and happiness

Rewards of life we earn.

Thank you for your Spiritual Strength

And for our thoughts to praise;

Thank you for your Infinite Love

That guides us through these days.

Acknowledgements

This life story of my father has been brewing for nine years, knowing he wanted it written, but never thinking I would be the one to do it. Somehow, it became clear that if I did not undertake this task, it probably would not occur. My three older siblings, now deceased did not "feel the calling," to write it. After working on the family tree in 2009 and 2011 on Ancestry.com, I decided to seriously think about writing it, which resulted in gathering reference materials from my older brother Bill Newell and my sister Diane Leary.

I extend my thanks to several individuals as I embarked on my mission to complete this biography of my father. The encouragement I received from my own children and from members of the Creative Writing group at Life Enrichment Center for the Arts in Tampa is paramount in my thoughts. Those individuals who gave guidance and direction are: Arlene Mariotti, Martin Newell, John Chaplick, Patricia McGehee, Mike Bartolotta, Robert Moore, Pam St. Mary, John E. Christ and Dr. Dr. Thayer. Their technical assistance and periodic evaluations made this document possible. I am grateful for their patience and guidance which gave me the confidence to complete this biography.

Table of Contents

A Seneca Praise iii

Acknowledgements iv

Table of Contents v

Introduction ix

Chapter 1: Struggle to Succeed in a White Man's World 1

Chapter 2: The "French Professor" 9

Armistice Day in Paris 10

Chapter 3: Courtship: A Fortunate Assimilation 21

Juggling Work and School 26

Chapter 4: "The Greatest Achievement of My Life" 27

Life Long Public Speaking Begins 32

Chapter 5: Pressing for More Reforms 35

Intolerable Conditions 35

New Endeavors 37

Chapter 6: Navigating the Great Depression Years 41

Back to School for a Master's Degree 42

Moving Turmoil 43

A Break in Routine 47

Searching for Opportunities 48

Chapter 7: A Waiting Game to Become a Civil Servant 51

Pursuing New Activities While Waiting 52

Chapter 8: Achievement Beyond Civil Service 57

v

Brooklyn to Long Island 60

Chapter 9: A Museum of His Own 63
"Long Island Express" 63

Chapter 10: Aiding World War II Effort 69
An Exciting Night with Bill Newell 69
War Engulfs the United States 72

Chapter 11: Working Again for Civil Service 73
Life at Fort H.G. Wright Army Base, Fisher's Island, N.Y. ... 73
1946 74
Life in the Fire Department 75

Chapter 12: A Rewarding Life as Professor Newell 77
Uplifted in Spirit in 1947 78

Chapter 13: National Recognition and Move to Tampa 81

Chapter 14: The Big "C" and Blindness 83
No Voice Now 84
Blindness 84
Relaxing at Last 85

Chapter 15: Retirement and European Adventures 87
European Adventures 89

Chapter 16: A Review of "Crime and Punishment" 91
Murder 93
More Travels 95

Chapter 17: Indian Nations Rise Up 97

Chapter 18: National Recognition on Origin of Thanksgiving
.... 101

Return to Tampa and the End of His Life 103

Summary of Life Events 105

Appendix I: Contributions of the American Indian to Modern Civilization by William B. Newell, 1939 (excerpts) 109

Appendix II: Message from William B. Newell 119

Appendix III: What I Believe About Jesus Christ 121

Appendix IV: North American Indian Traveling College Definitions 129

Notes 131

Introduction

At the beginning of the 20th Century, Native American Indians in New England and eastern Canada had largely been assimilated into white culture. However, there were resistant ones who continued to exist in mostly small groups living on "reservations." Some continued living in remote areas with little or no help from any governing body. Apathy prevailed among the white population of Americans and Canadians, towards Native Americans.

A few organizations emerged, concerned for their welfare. One such group was the General Federated Women's Clubs of western New York who in 1926 promoted measures that were constructive in character and beneficial for the Indians. They were aware that terms of Treaties were mostly destructive of the rights of the Indian; unjust and oppressive. They declared that this was contrary to the true spirit of Democracy. They resolved to heartily support all legislative measures which would grant to the Indian their full rights to include the right to land, legal and health protection and a modern education. Branches of the Federated Women's Clubs in other states promoted and established investigations into intolerable conditions on reservations. Many important pieces of legislations were passed during 1923-24 Congress. They made attempts at working with the United States Indian Bureau hoping that it would bring attention to dire situations that existed on reservations. It was a struggle due to indifference and prejudice held by authorities (governors, legislators, press affiliates). This state of affairs is still an on-going struggle today.

In 1926, my father formed the Society for the Propagation of Indian Welfare in New York State, and began publishing a quarterly journal, "The Six Nations" that he edited. At this time he was lay missionary on the Cattaraugus Indian Reservation where he ministered to the Seneca Indians. There were five aims of this society and journal.

1. Bring a better understanding between whites and Indians.
2. Bring to the attention of the government all unjust or unfair treatment of the Indians
3. Secure better educational facilities for the Indians on state reservations.
4. Study and solve the many Indian problems.
5. Back all fair legislation and oppose all unfair legislation affecting Indians.

This biography follows the journey of Professor William B. Newell aka Ta-lo-wah-ren-ha-gai, as he promoted the contributions of the American Indians to modern civilization. He referred himself as Rolling Thunder II after his father. He lectured to hundreds of Rotary, Kiwanis, women's clubs, high schools, men's clubs, church groups, and institutions of higher learning throughout his adult life. He hoped to quash the apathy that existed about Indians, and any negative attitude held about their intellectual capacity. He earnestly wanted to acquaint the general public about their contributions to society and worked all his adult life with the goal of improving the welfare of Indians everywhere.

For informational purposes this author explains that the Six Nations, comprised of Mohawk, Oneida, Onondaga, Cayuga, Seneca and Tuscarora nations call themselves the *Haudenosaune,* or People of the Longhouse. They meet as the Six Nations Iroquois Confederacy with 50 some chiefs of the nations gathering periodically for a grand council meeting. Historians say the confederacy founded between A.D. 1350 and 1600, was established by the man called the *Peacemaker*. The confederacy covered much of central and western New York State and eventually dispersed to a scattering of ever dwindling reservations on both sides of the United States/Canadian border. Syracuse, New York is one city central to these nations.

Chapter 1: Struggle to Succeed in a White Man's World

This is the true story of one Mohawk-Penobscot Indian who "ran against the tide" in his attempt to survive and educate himself so he could adequately provide for his family. In this process, he voraciously wished to educate and promote the good image of the Indian in the eyes of the white population. My father, William Benjamin Newell was born on December 17, 1892, in Boston, Massachusetts to Louisa Warionkwas Stump, a young Mohawk woman. Thus, he began his long struggle to be successful in the white man's world.

Louisa became proficient in shooting a rifle during her childhood and began performing in shows at age 17. She became known by three names during her career which are Texas Lillie, Rosy Gordon and Prairie Flower. She traveled with promoters of Wild West shows like Buffalo Bill's famous show.

Day after day she entered an arena shooting rosin balls out of the air which had been propelled by a mechanical device. The rosin balls were about the size of ping pong balls and she would shoot them out of the air, never missing one. At other times, she would ride on her horse in a prone position leaning backward-while shooting them. Louisa, born in New York City, but advertised as "the beautiful shooting star of the Lone Star State" traveled the northeastern United States and Canada. She was the daughter of a German immigrant, William Stump who served in the Army during the Civil War and Mohawk native, Ida Warionkwas. Since the Mohawks are a matriarchal society she is considered Iroquois.

Left alone and lost in the shadows of Louisa's performances, my father became invisible. Fortunately, his mother realized that show business was no place for a child. In the absence of any schools for Indian children on the reservations in the early 1900's, Louisa decided to enroll him at Saint Louis Convent in Montreal. He would get an education and study music. One can imagine the feeling of abandonment young William must have felt when his mother waved goodbye as she left him in the care of the nuns who probably saw him as a pitiful child. He was nine years old and remained there for two years, becoming indoctrinated in the Catholic religion.

He noted that he learned to fear God with all his heart and while he knew all the Latin responses by heart he did not understand what they meant. He thought he must have done well because he began serving at 5 o'clock (in the morning) mass. At that time even being confirmed and taking first communion did not make a very great impression on him. He elaborated that as time went on he had a sense of obligation and gradually continued as a practicing Catholic, for the next eight years. William's diary stated that he had become imbued with the idea that " God was watching every move I made and actually felt that He was angry with me when I did some imaginary wrong."

My father's diary tells of travels with his mother to see Queen Victoria in Montreal and then to attend the World's Fair in Buffalo, New York in 1901. However, this could not be considered a stable home life.

At age fifteen he began working for his uncle, Al E. Reed, who managed a Read-O-Scope in Maisonneuve, a suburb of Montreal, Canada, one of Montreal's first moving picture theaters, at a time they were all beginning to surface in North America, in 1907.

William began as an usher. When he became proficient, his uncle promoted him to projectionist; eventually, he rose to the level of First Class Projectionist. His uncle began to open theaters in other locations and then close them when they did not show a profit. I wonder about audience attendance, since this came before air-conditioning. William became Chief Projectionist at the Alexandra Theater by the time he had reached the age of majority and had two eighteen year- old assistants.

Looking back to the summer of 1911, when his uncle closed one of his theaters, my father went to work with 700 Indians from the Cauganawaga Indian Reservation in the Cobalt Silver Mines, Ontario, Canada. He worked there three months with Paul Jacobs whose brother, Joseph, later married my aunt, Malvina. William recorded in his journal that he nearly cut off his big toe on the right foot while chopping wood for the boiler with a double bladed axe. At 18 years old, that must have been a frightening experience!

In 1914, when he had saved $500 (not a paltry sum in those days), his uncle cajoled him into investing in yet another theater in Toronto. This proved to be a mistake because they only operated for about four weeks when the theater failed! William thought, at some point that his uncle had taken advantage of him and his naivety.

My father met his father for the first time since his birth in September 1914, when he traveled to his father's Quaker Ridge farm located in rural New York having had no contact with him prior to that time. It is apparent that his mother, Louisa, and Louis Belmont Newell never shared a married life together. She met him as the proprietor of Rolling Thunder's Kiowa Medicine and Vaudeville Company, a traveling- show from Steamburg, New York, where she worked for him. People addressed him as "Dr. Newell", creator of numerous herbal remedies which he developed at his farm. An eager public that clamored for solutions to their everyday aches and pains, became his customers.

Louis B. Newell known as Rolling Thunder, my grandfather, a Penobscot Indian, sometimes claimed to be of Kiowa heritage, a western tribe. He was born to Thomas Newell and Marie Parsons of Indian Island, Old Town, Maine. Both were Penobscot natives. My grandfather married at least three times; the last marriage to Jeanne(Jennie) Congleton, with her age being 20; the doctor, 52. Dissension among her relatives occurred because of the differences in their ages, but the marriage proved to be long- lasting, producing one son, Paul Newell. Jennie entertained William in later years when William brought his own family to visit his father at the farm.

"Dr." Newell with his traveling show went to all parts of the United States, Canada and Mexico until age 79. He played the violin while his wife, Jennie, accompanied him, playing the organ to entertain the audience before selling his remedies.

A printed flyer mentions Texas Lillie's Sure Shot Indian Blood Purifier tonic; promoting it as a remedy for blood, liver, stomach and kidney diseases when taken one tablespoon in a glass of water, 3 times a day before eating. He prepared it from carefully selected roots, barks, and herbs. His fly bill advertisement states "The Great Spirit is kind – teaching his creatures to know what is good for them. The real Natives of America have learned many good medicines from the beasts, fowls, fishes and even from the insignificant insects themselves."

Dr. Newell had medicines for costiveness, indigestion, dyspepsia, flatulence, headache, cold stomach, cough, stomach pain, jaundice, and dropsy. After he stopped his traveling show numerous customers sought him out at his farm to buy his tonics.

As William's daughter, I pose this question to the reader: how did this Indian child who led the nomadic life of an orphan, come to distinguish himself to the extent that he became included in Who's Who in The East, Who's Who in American Education, Who's Who in New England, Who's Who in The South and lastly, Who's Who in America (1964-1965)? The answer might be that sometime in 1914, while attempting to configure the focal lens distance while operating the motion picture machine, he realized that he was illiterate. He had picked up a little reading and writing, but math remained a mystery. He did not understand the use of capital letters and punctuation marks. My father, embarrassed at times, began to realize he could be a more productive citizen by obtaining an education even though he could earn $35.00 for a 7day week, as a first-class projectionist.

He became a member of the International Alliance of Theatrical, Stage Employees local union and vice president as well. Unhappy with his status, he wrote in his diary: "This handicap caused me to decide to go to school, so in the fall of 1914, I entered Fort Covington New York Union School, four miles from my home on the St. Regis Indian Reservation, in Franklin County."

Local principal, Dr. Glen A. Sealy, tested William, and told him that he had the equivalent of a 4th grade education, but he would permit him to enter with the fourth grade students, although by this time he was almost 22years old. William continues, "After a few weeks they knew my efforts were in earnest and my desire to secure an education so keen. . . I would be advanced to 7th grade. When mid-year examinations were held in January, I passed all the work with honors, having had over 90% in all final papers."

William continued to excel and immediately went into high school, passing one full year of work in half a year. He persevered for another year and continued to work as a projectionist. Around this time he became a member of the fraternal Independent Order of Odd Fellows in Lodge Lafayette #15 of Montreal. Founded in England in the 18th century, this organization had as their motto: "Friendship, Love and Truth," which also describes its purpose. It was important to him. It is still an active organization today striving to make the world a better place by giving aid to those who need it.

So, how did he become so motivated considering his childhood environment? Both of his parents could read and write quite well, but I doubt that either one of them was the stimulus. I believe the answer lies with Dr. Sealy who became his mentor and lifelong friend encouraging him to excel in all his educational pursuits. (Photo: William and Celina with Dr. Glen Sealy)

Chapter 2: The "French Professor"

At the onset of World War One, William felt compelled to join the fight against the Germans and give his support to our nation by joining the American Expeditionary Forces. He traveled to Jamestown, New York and enlisted in the U.S. Army. His platoon, stationed at Fort Slocum, New York, found themselves in Madison Barracks while they waited to be deployed in the fall of 1917. His 500 comrades labeled him the "French professor." William grew up communicating in both French and English with his relatives.

A cryptic comment from his diary tells us on November 10th. 1917, they "left Madison Barracks in the middle of the night with all lights extinguished, car windows drawn so that no one could see this event. Embarked at Hoboken in the early dawn for France."

Attached to the 42nd Division, my father stayed in Paris for the duration of the war, assigned to interpret French for Captain Osborne, the general purchasing agent for the American Expeditionary Forces with his living quarters at the Champs-Elysees Hotel.

During 1918, the flu pandemic (named the Spanish Flu) broke out and spread to all parts of the world. Unusually virulent, it mostly affected healthy young adults in contrast to most influenza outbreaks which predominately affect juvenile, elderly or those with weakened immune systems; between 50 and 100 million people died, making it one of the deadliest natural disasters in human history. In March 1918, William contracted the flu and spent six weeks confined at the American Red Cross Hospital located at 6 Rue Piccini in Paris. He considered himself one of the fortunate ones.

In an assignment that he wrote during his enrollment in an English class at Syracuse University after World War I, my father described the bedlam that broke out on the streets of Paris on Armistice Day:

Armistice Day in Paris

"Paris with its great broad streets and boulevards, its beautiful parks and gardens, was the scene of a great unofficial celebration on that memorable day, the eleventh of November. It was my good fortune to have been there and to have witnessed some of the things that took place on that date. To give you an exact picture of Paris as it was on that day is a task for some great writer but I am going to make an attempt to describe some of the most important features that took place that day.

During the last four years of that war the people of Paris led a very secluded life and all signs of gaiety and pleasure were laid aside. For four years the city had been clothed in mourning and everything had been dreary and black. The young men were all gone, the old men were putting up a last resistance, and the very old people remained at home with the very young, behind closed shutters and drawn curtains. All that they could do was to pray that the absent son or father would soon come home to stay for the last time. For four years they kept those shutters closed even on the hottest summer day. For four years they kept in the dark, but the day was not far off when their prayers were to be answered and that dark period was to end and those shutters that remained always closed were to fly open and the free bright sunshine was again to be theirs. That day was fast approaching and was to come sooner than expected. But the very fact that that day was so near did not cause these people to brighten up the least. They had heard too many wild rumors during those four years and were not to be fooled even by such a rumor as the war being over. So that when the morning of the eleventh of November arrived there was no change in the appearance of the city.

It was two minutes to eleven and I stood listening for the signal that was to let the peoples of the world know that the papers had been signed which meant the end of hostilities. I did not wait long before I heard erroneous firing in the distance, and this was followed up by the wildest excitement and noise. Bells were ringing, whistles were blowing and people were running through the streets shouting with the wildest joy. Elderly ladies rushed up to me with tears of joy in their eyes and thanked me for the part that America had played in the war.

Young girls threw their arms about every soldier that they met. And those shutters that had been closed for four years; those shutters that had kept the sunshine out were thrown open wide, and bright smiling faces appeared on all sides. The houses that had had the appearance of being empty and un-occupied took on the brightest colors and life seemed to prevail everywhere.

Flags began to appear from all the windows and doors of every house in Paris. A stampede was made on the flag stores and within half an hour after the rush began it was impossible to buy a flag of any description. Where flags could not be bought buntings of all colors were used instead. In the business districts the decorations were so thickly hung that the stores and buildings were completely hidden from view. The business people were expecting this day and were prepared to decorate and invest money in making a big display.

Crowds began to gather in the public squares and on the grand boulevards. People came into Paris from all the surrounding districts and it was not long before the streets and public places were densely crowded with the wild multitude. No one worked that afternoon. Everyone took a holiday. All of the offices and factories were closed and the people turned loose-free to do as they pleased. As I hurried along with the crowds I was saluted and thanked time and time again by the people. As we drew near the Place de la Concord the crowds began to grow thicker and by the time I set foot on the rue Royal, the street which leads to the grand boulevard from the southern part of the city, the crowds became so dense that it was quite difficult to go forward. After arriving on the grand boulevard, it was impossible to move in any direction that you would choose, but you were compelled to follow the moving mass of humanity as it surged this way and that way. It took me half an hour to go one block and during that time I thought that I would never get out of that wild mob of cheering people. Little children were in danger of losing their lives and I am sure many were hurt although I did not see any accidents. I saw a woman faint within six feet of me from the rush and it is a miracle that some were not killed! It was not until along towards six o'clock that the crowd loosened up so that a person could walk along without being crushed.

On all sides, could be heard the shouts of people crying, "Vive l'Amerique" and "Vive le Allies." The American soldiers who happened to be in the crowds that day were heroes, one and all. People embraced them and showered them with flowers and carried them on their shoulders. Pretty Parisienne girls made many a bashful boy blush by their embraces. The cry of "Vive l'Amerique" was on all tongues. There is no question about the appreciation of the French people towards the aid of America. It was shown that day.

Everything in the way of celebrating was done by the young people. Some soldiers and girls attached ropes to some of the captured German cannons that were on display at the Place de la Concord and dragged them through the streets singing and yelling on the top of their voices. Some pretty girl would be sitting on the cannon waving a flag and crying, "Vive les Allies." Crowds of boys and girls gathered in groups and went running thru the streets hand in hand. Whenever they spied any American they would surround him and not allow him out of the circle until he had kissed every girl in the circle. Very few tried to escape these circles and in fact many did not wait for the next circle but threw their arms around the first girl they met. There were hundreds of parades got up by different gangs of soldiers. Someone with a flag would start off and in a minute, he would have a hundred with him and by the time he was gone a block he would have a thousand behind him. They would march along with the stars and stripes and the French flag nearly always was with it. The funniest thing of all was to see some well-known girls wearing the hats of YMCA men. But many things were overlooked that day. Such as the two happy MP's that I saw trying to walk straight, and the Lieutenant who wanted to sell his bars for five francs, and the buck sergeant who was wearing eagles on his shoulders. The climax of the evening was when six thousand Americans under Colonel Johnson formed at the Place de Glace and started for the boulevards. By the time we had reached the main boulevard we had picked up a few thousand more and our parade got so large that it lost itself on the boulevard and was split up by the mingling of the thousands. It was now about midnight and I had put in a very strenuous day of it so I joined the next parade going to my way of thinking which was to go home to rest.

I reached my barracks and found that I was the first one to come home. But it was not long before the next man came in all "tired out," with the day's experience. We were both asleep by two o'clock when someone turned the light on and let out a yell. "Vive l'Amerique," he said and came staggering over to my bed with a glass of champagne in his hand. He insisted that I drink it claiming he had carried it six blocks and would not be refused. I refused; he drank the wine, swearing that he was no longer my friend. All of this was said in French as he would not use a single word of English. I managed to get him to bed and we three finally got to sleep again when about 3 am someone else came in and awakened us by his cry of "Vive l'Amerique." It is needless for me to say that I did not get any sleep that night or for any night for the following week.

I will never forget as long as I live, the days of the Armistice that I spent in Paris and I would not take a million dollars for my experiences there that day."

On December 14, 1918, William braved huge crowds of Parisians who had gathered at the Place de la Concord to get a glimpse of President Woodrow Wilson on his visit to the Paris Peace Conference. The words **Vive Wilson** outlined with electric lights hung over the street. William had a photo of this scene in his records and wrote at the top:

"I was here when this photo was taken."

A special bulletin issued to American Expeditionary Forces announced the opening of a university for those in the military who wished to pursue their education while awaiting return to the states. William immediately registered for courses at this university and for the next three months studied liberal arts at Beaune, France located 172 miles south of Paris, completing his high school work.

One day while at Beaune he became inspired to have every man in his platoon sign his name and address in what amounted to an "autograph" book asking them to express their sentiments about being in the army. What ensued is a log of humourous thoughts and anecdotes.

These signings, many of which were expressed in verse are a testament to the frustrations the soldiers were feeling when they were homesick and anxiously waiting for a ship to take them home to the USA.

Here are some of those signatures that bring insight into that year of 1919:

James Gleagan, 264 Forest Ave. Bangor, Maine

    Little drops of powder.

    Little dabs of paint

    Make the French girls complexions

    Look what it ain't.

Ellsworth Escott, Houtzdale, Pennsylvania

    Remember those halcyon days at the University of Beaune.

Harry J. Brown, 89 Beckwith Place, Rutherford, New Jersey, USA

    The Frenchman likes his native wine,

    The German likes his beer

    The Englishman likes his whiskey straight

    Because it gives him dizziness

    The Americans having no choice left, drinks

    The whole d____ business!

G.A. Sahli, 204 Whiton St. Whitewater, Wisconsin

"And when shall we finish that chess tournament?"

Robert G. Linderman, Ashton, Idaho

"Paris has won your heart

With its beautiful gardens & fountains

But mine shall ever be in Idaho

"The Gem of the Rocky Mountains.'"

Wm J. Keary, 1030 Street, New York City

"I have no pain dear mother,

Though I am so very dry

Connect me with the brewery

And leave me there to die."

Bruce G. McAbery, 838 35th St. Des Moines, Iowa

"Here's to the "frog" with whom we love to

Quarrel. When we get back to the good old USA

In this one respect, we shall sorrow."

William H. Rowe, Beacon, Michigan

The American's name is Can-can

The Frenchman's name is "Frog"

The freeman's name is "civilian"

But the soldier's status is "dog"

Wei Yuen Char, 457 N. King St. Honolulu, Hawaii

"You may have your Golden Gate

Broadway may be fine;

But Honolulu, the paradise of the Pacific

Is the place for mine"

J.W. Sanders, Richburg, South Carolina

"There has been many a slip between the AEF and a ship,

But when we see the Statue of Liberty, the bow will dip."

Among the signatures I found this Soldier's Prayer:

Our father, who art in Washington,

Baker be they name, Thy cobles come they will be done,

In Paris as in Beaune. Give us this month our long delayed pay,

And forgive us our AWOL's as we forgive the Mess Sergeant,

The Bugler and the YMCA. Leave us not in the army of Occupation,

But deliver us from another service ship for thine is any army of MP's,

QM's and field decks forever and ever. Amen

An Italian fruit ship, Calamarias, transported my father and his comrades home to America arriving on July 5, 1919. William was honorably discharged on July 16, 1919, with the rank of Sergeant after serving his country in France for twenty-one months.

Chapter 3: Courtship: A Fortunate Assimilation

The foremost thought on William's mind as he returned to civilian life was to further his education by earning a degree from Syracuse University. I know he wanted to improve his life and prove to humanity that an Indian could indeed learn beyond the 4th grade as the rest of the world then believed. He intended to achieve this goal. However, love would intervene.

Upon his arrival home, he went first to see his mother (Louisa), at the St. Regis Reservation aka Akwesasne Reserve along the St. Lawrence River. He then visited Celina Canadian, 18, whom he had met before the war, at an ice cream parlor. The story of their first meeting as told by Celina (the author's mother) is that she and her friends including a Joe Bell were at an ice cream establishment when she first met my father. She gave William a rosebud from the flowers she was holding which made Joe so jealous and angry, he stormed out. William ended up paying for five sundaes when her friends left without paying the tab. Thus, began their lifelong relationship. She was 16 and he was nearly 26 when, evidently, romantic feelings began to develop. She later slipped out of her home without her parents' knowledge to bid William adieu at the train station when he left for France.

It was clear to William that Celina's native heritage made an impression on him. Celina, one of five daughters of John A. and Marie Canadian grew up around Montreal, Canada, and was born on Kahwanake Indian Reservation, which is located across the St

Lawrence River, and Montreal. Her Iroquois lineage goes back to include Chief Joseph Delisle, a Mohawk chief who lived in the 1850's.

A rather infamous grandfather is a Scotsman by the name of Gervase/ Jarvis McComber, who married two or three times to Indian women. He fathered 26 children as documented in the book "Gervase Macomber and His 26 Children in Kahnawake, (Caughnawaga)" by John Masiewicz, published in 2016. One of them was my maternal grandmother, the 18th child of Gervase, Marie Malvina, born in February 1844.

My most famous great-grandfather is John Baptist Canadien, aka "Big John," a foremost Iroquois guide, frontiersman, and an extraordinary athlete. He captained an exhibition Lacrosse team that toured in the British Isles and Australia in 1876. At nearly six feet tall, he sported a bushy mustache and had silvery hair. His arms and hands were massive. Robust and healthy even at 78 years of age, he was a fearless explorer. A twinkle in his eye bespoke his quick wit and sensitive perception of the moment. The Canadian newspapers often reported on his activities.

He had the extreme honor of being presented to Queen Victoria, "the good mother," as he referred to her thereafter. The story that evolved is after he had shaken her hand to the horror of on-lookers, he leaned forward to plant a light kiss on her cheek. The Queen took this gesture in good stride. He vowed he would "never wash his hand again." Of course, he later changed his mind. He kept a gold framed autographed photo of her Majesty which she had given to him on the wall of his rustic pioneer home – once described by a Montreal Herald newspaper reporter as "rugged and weathered like himself."

His expertise in canoeing led to his becoming the lead guide to British field agent, Marshall Wolseley in his 1870's explorations of the Red River country of western Canada; then, largely uncharted. Again, selected for a journey to Egypt by the same General Wolseley, he assisted in fighting the Turkish Dervishes.

"Big John" led 81 Native American boatmen up the treacherous cataracts of the Nile River transporting troops and supplies in a failed expedition. They toiled under the grueling sun of the Sudan to assist the British Empire. They received lavish praise from both houses of the British Parliament. The city of Montreal warmly welcomed the men home with a festive celebration in 1884.

An unnamed newspaper reporter, described "Big John" as the champion "rapids runner" of the world. In his more vigorous days, his powerful arms, athletic ability and daring spirit often led him to "shoot the Lachine Rapids" in a specially constructed rowboat, that he had built. For several years, postcards were issued and sold which pictured him with four companions in this vessel. In the year 1915, he told the Montreal Star newspaper that he would no longer take the trip down the rapids on the upcoming New Year's Day, saying "my arms are now too weak to hold up any longer the banner of the rapids championship." Nearing 75 years of age; he knew when to quit.

Many years earlier he helped guide steamships that came down from upper Canada, safely through the foaming rapids. People loved to observe him in his colorful regalia, push off from shore and head for the steamer which he boarded and offered his services to the captain of the ship. His generous nature and charm made him welcome everywhere.

I have a formal family portrait taken in later years which included his wife, Marie and their seven grown sons and daughter. All of them are dressed in suits and ties and looked like lawyers and judges. No-one would ever think they were Indians. By this time, it appears they had assimilated into white society. It could be said, that this photograph – left for his heirs and history could be a testament to his success and prosperity.

An unknown benefactor, selected Celina's father, John A. Canadian to receive an education at prestigious Oxford University. He lived in Liverpool, England for a few years, before returning to Montreal, Canada to work for the Canadian Pacific Railway, where he raised a family of five girls and one boy. This information is told to acquaint the reader of the heritage of Celina and the importance it held for William as their relationship began to evolve in 1919.

The predominant thought on William's mind in the fall of 1919 was to get enrolled in college, at Syracuse University. He met with Dean Peck and convinced him to allow himself to be a "pay as you go" student. Officials agreed so long as he could prove himself by succeeding in his classes. Syracuse University had never allowed this unheard of arrangement before that time.

Next, William decided to pay a visit to see his father on his farm in rural New York. He wanted to share

Rolling Thunder's farmhouse at Cold Spring, N.Y. or Steamburg, N.Y. and the Newell's first automobile, purchased for Aunt Emma for $125.00

his enrollment news with him. Unfortunately, his father was on the road with his medicine show in Kinzu,

Pennsylvania. On the 26th of July, he did find his father at home who told him he had deeded William 700 acres of land on the Penobscot Old Town Reservation, a statement which proved to be a myth.

Juggling Work and School

William's first day as a Freshman student at Syracuse University must have been some-what overwhelming as he notes in his diary, "I enrolled in school with only $6.25 in my pocket ending up with $1.25 as I started working my way through college."

How he earned $60 to $70 a week "is a story in itself." He remarked, "I became night watchman in the gym for $18; made $6 on Saturday nights washing out the swimming pool; preached as a lay reader on Sundays at churches in Homer and Marathon, New York for $11 and became employed as a sports writer for the Syracuse Post Standard for two years, transferring to the Syracuse Herald after that for three years." He specialized in reporting on the game of Lacrosse and received between $10 and $25 each week for that endeavor. This author wonders how he found time to study, with all those jobs.

In October of the year 1919, we find him living at the Gibbs residence at 1651 East Lafayette Street while he continued with his classes at Syracuse. Apparently, two sisters who performed in a show business endeavor were friends of William and they allowed William to keep the house by himself while they were out of town. There are photos of them in the family photo album.

Chapter 4: "The Greatest Achievement of My Life"

On November 13th, November 1921 William had his first opportunity to express his strong opinions regarding the education of Indians to the large audience of the New York State Welfare Society. Although still a student, he had been elected a Conciliator for the St Regis Mohawk Nation and therefore got the opportunity to speak before many prominent educators. These included the Director of New York State Indian Schools, Mr. A.C. Hill and Dr. Richard Pratt, founder of the Carlisle Indian Industrial School in Carlisle, Pennsylvania.

To acquaint the reader, this Carlisle Indian boarding school had over 10,000 Native American children in attendance between 1879 and 1918, from 140 tribes. Sponsored by the United States federal government, children were forced to leave their families at young ages, give up their cultures, languages, religion and even had to change their names, which did great psychological damage to many of them. Discipline was strict and consistent, administered in military tradition and those who did not adjust often ran away in attempts to return to their homes. It was a tragic philosophy the white population held that they must "kill the Indian: save the Man." It was their hope to assimilate all Indians as rapidly as possible into American culture, thus saving them from eventual extinction.

William reported to the grand audience, "For thirty years not a single move was made to improve the educational facilities of the Indians living on Indian Reservations in all of New York State." The Rochester Telegram and other newspapers quoted my father in their papers the next day. They quoted him: "The educational system today is disgraceful. The highest grade an Indian can get on the reservation is fourth grade, and after he has reached the fourth grade they keep him there until he gets tired and drops out." Reporters left out this quote however: "When a man has spent 30 years or more trying to educate Indians and then actually believed that an Indian did not have the intelligence to go beyond the fourth grade, it is high time he retired and went on pension."

Director, A.C. Hill, sitting in about the 5th row when William spoke, looked straight at him. Hill reportedly hung his head in shame. Shortly thereafter he resigned his position and a Dr. Hague replaced him.

My father always thought this was one of the greatest achievements of his life as he continued to push for reforms for the Indians. In May 1920, a new organization had formed when various leaders met in Syracuse, named the Indian Welfare Society of New York, with Dr. Arthur C. Parker, leading Indian authority, president. Rev. Louis Bruce, William and two other Mohawks were also elected to represent the Mohawks. Many others from various reservations also helped to complete this new organization. My father resolved to work tirelessly on this endeavor and said: "I became an Indian fighter from this day on. I did not quit insisting that all of the schools of New York raise the levels for Indians to 8th grade."

Articles appeared in the newspapers in Syracuse, Buffalo and Rochester about these efforts. William continued to emphasize the deficient conditions in the Indian schools and remembered an incident that occurred in 1915-five years prior when he met a tobacco chewing principal at Hogansburg School. His disgusting appearance; his total indifference to the welfare of the pupils and the type of teachers under him were repulsive in every respect.

This must have been the catalyst that compelled William to try and improve conditions for Indian children. I am reminded that compassion is based on others' fundamental rights to be happy and overcome suffering. It is a fact that Indians were suffering to a large extent as documented by journals that were published during the 1920's.

My father continued to pay his tuition in dribs and drabs. He frequently mentioned paying $10 here and $20 there as he earned money from different sources. In January 1921, he worked for room and board at Dr. Mahoney's at 121 Green Street in Syracuse taking care of the furnace, shoveling snow off the walkways and guarding the house when the doctor and his wife left the premises. He studied much of the time. He notes that he received a grant of $100 for tuition from the education fund for veterans from the YMCA.

Against the advice of his father, William began visiting Celina and they decided to get married. They married on August 22, 1921, at St. James Methodist Church on St. Catherine Street in Montreal, Canada.

Every summer during his undergraduate days at Syracuse, together, they sold genuine Mohawk Indian baskets, moccasins, beaded bags and other articles created on the reservation at a resort at Lake Chautauqua, the Finger Lakes region of New York, to earn money for his tuition. Going to the market meant getting up at 3:30 a.m. and traveling six miles where William and Celina sold between $200 and $300 worth of Indian goods two or three mornings each week, averaging $100 a week.

An article appeared in one newspaper attesting to the fact that he sold Indian moccasins to the sorority girls at the university. I think the newspaper was looking for a human interest story, plus he was a reporter for that same newspaper.

In September 1921, my father decided to petition the Dean of Liberal Arts to drop out of college for one year. It was granted. It is apparent to me that the strain of working his way through college was exacerbated by setting up housekeeping with his wife or "little sweetheart" as he often referred to my mother.

On New Year's Day, 1922, his diary reveals that William and Celina were visiting his mother in Massena, New York, when Celina became ill and bedridden. He had to leave them however and return to Syracuse to attend classes and to their rented room from a "nice" English lady, a Mrs. Cook.

On January 9th Celina returned from Massena and went to see Dr. Burrows. He could not determine her illness so he referred her to the doctor from Crouse Irving Hospital. Two days later they transported her to the hospital in severe pain where she had a miscarriage. She was nearly four months pregnant. William had dinner with his "little sweetheart" at the hospital where a nurse in attendance tried to cheer them up by telling them they would have twins next time. Daddy reports feeling lonesome and anxious for the day she would be released and come home to him.

While my mother slowly recuperated, my father came down with a case of shingles. Nevertheless, he was elated to have her back home with him. He began a job with Mr. Gere & Company, selling coal at $25 per week. They had business cards printed up for him, but when they couldn't deliver the orders he had obtained, he began performing Easy Washing Machine demonstrations at $35 a week instead. He continued to write stories about the Indian School situation in his ongoing quest for better standards which appeared in various newspapers.

In the summer of 1923, my parents moved to Bemus Point, New York where they opened a gift shop called "Rolling Thunder's Art & Gift Shop." This, a new business venture had a business card stating "The Newer Art Creations Make Delightful Decorations." To their satisfaction, one summer they sold $6,000 worth of Indian objects. At the end of that year William splurged by purchasing a Muskrat "Hudson Seal" fur coat for Celina, paying $100 cash. She valued it for many years.

Life Long Public Speaking Begins

William began to receive speaking invitations from various civic organizations in 1923. On July 19th William and Celina went to Buffalo, N.Y., where he spoke to 500 members of the Rotary Club in the main dining room of Hotel Statler. Many of those who heard him speak were impressed and stated they would never forget his speech. Ten years later he met one of those individuals. William reiterates the story in his notes this way: On October 19, 1933, I spoke before the Philadelphia Rotary Club and during the luncheon I sat next to a gentleman whose name I did not get. During the conversation, he casually told me that the best talk he ever heard was given by a young Indian man. His wife was along with him (the only woman present at the luncheon). I was a little embarrassed as he told me this story, but when he finished telling me about the remarkable talk he had heard, I leaned over and said, "I must tell you that it was me you heard."

My father graduated from Syracuse in June 1924 with a degree in philosophy and minor in French. Again, more publicity for the Newell family with the Syracuse Herald picturing his father Rolling Thunder, age 81, his seventh month old son, William Albert David Newell in a cradleboard, and my father in his cap and gown.

His family which will in time include five children, began in 1923. The Syracuse Herald ran a photo of mother and son with the headline: *Rolling*

Thunder's Papoose to be Christened U-Ha-Hi-O, which means Straight Path. This announcement ran on October 25th, 1923.

Chapter 5: Pressing for More Reforms

As my father neared the end of his studies at Syracuse University he decided that he did indeed want to set an example for his people as well as promote the welfare of the Indians. He decided to become a Protestant Episcopal missionary for the diocese of western New York for a period of four years, lasting from September 1924 through 1928. The Newell family moved onto the Cattaraugus Reservation, near Buffalo, New York, assisting the Seneca Indians during those four years.

In June of 1924, several religious organizations ran missions on Indian reservations over the country, including New York State. Among these were Methodist, Baptist, Episcopalian and Presbyterian denominations. They had all written letters to my father and met with him to entice him to work among the Indians.

Intolerable Conditions

William lamented that while there were Indian welfare organizations working for justice for the Indians on federal reservations, New York State Indians had been left to live in intolerable conditions. For one thing, he felt that the New York state schools should require all teachers to hold a certificate and not be allowed to teach Indians without one as they were then allowed to do. He discovered as he worked with the children and families on the Cattaraugus Reservation, most had never been given a medical examination.

He personally witnessed a young boy in a classroom lying on his desk apparently asleep, but was told by his teacher, "He is dying." When the shock of her statement sunk in and after she explained the nature of the boy's disease, the teacher was asked why she allowed a boy dying of tuberculosis to mingle with the other children in the school. She retorted, "What difference does it make? They all have it!"

My father immediately removed the child and took him to a hospital and then scheduled and brought in the Buffalo Tuberculosis Association to hold a clinic at this school. Five others were also found tubercular that year. He continued to transport a great number of sick Indians to a hospital for treatment during the ensuing years. He was reprimanded during his first year as a missionary by the Board of Missions for his "crusader tactics." (See Appendix IV What I Believe About Jesus Christ)

He told an appalling story about a 90 year- old man who had stayed at his home with his leg hurting. He kept it covered with several overcoats. My father was determined to get the old man up. He found that his foot was bothering him and insisted on taking him to the hospital. When the medical attendant took the man's shoe off his toes came off with it. Gangrene had set in.

Three more Tuberculosis clinics were held on New York reservations in 1924 where 150 children were examined. He also negotiated with the American Red Cross of Buffalo to hold a dental clinic that 15 children attended. One little girl had 14 cavities; well on her way to losing all her teeth. In one district during the year 1925, there were five deaths caused by Tuberculosis. Apparently, Tuberculosis presented itself as a huge problem elsewhere in the United States, as well.

A public health supervising nurse on the nearby Onondaga Reservation reported that public health work had begun and they had a doctor with office hours three times a week. They also began providing prenatal and dental clinics as well. Health films were shown by the New York State Department of Health. Tuberculosis clinics were starting to be held twice a year with a spirit of good will and cooperation being seen on that reservation. Continuing efforts heartened my father.

New Endeavors

My father entered Delany Divinity School in September 1924, located in Buffalo, New York, but did not totally complete his studies there. He continued to

Will D. Newell was a missionary among the Seneca Indians on the Cattaraugus Indian Reservation N.Y. from 1924 thru 1928. Here is pictured a group of children that he escorted to Niagra Falls in 1925.

Seneca Indians from Cattaraugus Indian Reservation, N.Y. 1925

minister to the Indians on the Cattaraugus Reservation and to expose the children to new experiences to enrich their lives, such as a field trip to see Niagara Falls. His own family began to grow with another son, Frederick, Louis Newell born in 1925 and a daughter, Dorothy Mae Newell born in 1927.

During the years at Cattaraugus Reservation, he remained dedicated to the cause of promoting Indians, organizing the Six Nations Association, New York's most influential welfare society. It included the following nations: Mohawk, (keepers of the eastern door), Seneca, (keepers of the western door), Onondaga, (keepers of the central fire), and the Oneida, Cayuga, and Tuscarora Indian nations.

He inaugurated a quarterly journal, titled, "The Six Nations," which published news about New York Indians and of those on other reservations around the nation. The aims were: (1) bring about a better understanding between Indians and Whites, (2) bring to attention to the government all unjust or unfair treatment of Indians, (3) secure better educational facilities for Indians on state reservations, (4) study and solve many Indian problems, and (5) back all fair legislation and oppose all unfair legislation affecting Indians.

My father, the founder of this society edited this journal during the four years he lived there. The journal itself published information about the General Federated Women's Clubs concerning activities of American Indians in other locations in the United States, along with editorials by authorities and reports about upcoming legislation that could affect Indians.

In 1923, William gave his first lecture at the Chautauqua Institution before 1,200 women in the Hall of Philosophy. The following day, The Chautauqua Daily carried what my father described as "a nice article on my lecture." Thus, began thirty years of lecturing on the American Indian and the contributions that were made by them.

He notes at one point that "I have spoken to 46 Rotary clubs, 22 Kiwanis, 8 women's clubs, 56 high schools, 22 men's clubs, 43 institutions of higher learning and some 50 special interest groups." My father began to collect Stereoscope Lantern slides on Indian Life which included 45 famous American Indians. He eventually gathered 500 of these slides which he used to illustrate the talks he gave to civic, school and other groups throughout the northeast. These came before the advancement of films and videos. Some of these topics were: Famous American Indians, American Indian Inventions, American Indian Art, American Indian Agriculture, and Architecture. Lecturing became a way of life, one he used to support his family for many, many years. This author believes that her father must have had a charismatic way of speaking to his audience by the positive responses he received.

The General Federated Women's Clubs adopted a resolution in 1926, published in The Six Nations Quarterly supporting all legislation to grant full rights, including the right to own land, to legal protection, to health protection, and a modern education for the Indians while protesting any measures which rob the Indian of his constitutional rights and the protection to which every American citizen is entitled. This organization supported any measures to benefit the Indians and abhorred unjust treaties if they were oppressive and contrary to the true spirit of American democracy.

Collecting books for his library became his passion. He proudly amassed over 1,500 volumes of books in ethnology, archaeology, and anthropology, which he offered for use as reference material to writers and educators in the years that followed. All were non-fiction and were historical in nature. Eventually, most of these were given to the University of Florida by my father. Although I personally placed a number of his reference materials with Akwesasne Cultural Center, Hogansburg, New York, in 2011.

My father wanted to educate the public about the status of the Indian people and their accomplishments in the hopes that they would not be viewed as inferior to the white man, and could even be admired for who they were. He eventually realized that he was not held as an equal to the white man when he accepted government Civil Service work, only to be disappointed and disillusioned in where that led him. Government bureaucracy and prejudice were apparent which I will enlighten you about later in this story of his life.

He had also lectured at the New York Historical Society by this time and became a regular speaker for the prestigious Pratt Art Institute a few years later.

Chapter 6: Navigating the Great Depression Years

In September 1928, the Episcopal Missionary Department could no longer afford to maintain a resident missionary so the mission closed at Cattaraugus Reservation. William's only income came from lecturing. One day while giving a talk before the Brooklyn Kiwanis Club at Hotel St. George he announced that he could be available for any position that might guarantee him a future. Five men left their business cards one of which came from the Magnuson Products Corporation. He met with management who hired him immediately as a sales representative. Within two months Daddy became this company's star salesman, selling industrial cleaning products. He worked for this firm for two and one- half years. However, as the Great Depression began, the company put him on straight commission in August of 1931. The company withdrew the $75 per week he was earning due to falling sales. This forced William to resign.

Between 1931 and 1933 William and Celina and their family of three children, faced hard times. I recall my parents telling me about a tea room they ran in a building that had been a bowling alley, partitioning off a portion of it for living quarters and the remainder became a tea room.

My mother did all the cooking, baking, serving and dishwashing. Their customers were wealthy individuals, vacationing in the Finger Lakes area of New York near Lake Chautauqua, and the musicians who performed at establishments there. They would stop after their parties and events for a cup of coffee and a slice of my mother's freshly baked pies. My father notes in his diary that he felt grateful for his "good wife" who managed to keep them going at a time when relief amounted to $2.50 a week! I recall my mother reminiscing about the trying times of surviving the Great Depression. She never seemed to speak with regret but more with the satisfaction that our family survived just fine. I assume Daddy took care of the bills and the children.

He kept corresponding by mail with prospective employers. My mother, the eternal optimist, would encourage my father to try new opportunities. Those days gave them the resolve to live life with fortitude and an independent spirit while enthusiastically raising a family.

Back to School for a Master's Degree

After surviving the bitterly cold winter of 1932, William decided he needed to further his education by getting a master's degree in Sociology with the idea of getting into the United States Indian Service as a Social Worker or in some other capacity. With the assistance of friends, he secured a $1,000 scholarship and a loan of $250. He used this to move his family to Philadelphia. He had decided to enter the graduate department of the University of Pennsylvania. This prestigious institution was founded by Benjamin Franklin.

My father records that he hitch-hiked from Jamestown, New York to Philadelphia in the fall of 1933 to complete arrangements to attend graduate school in the Sociology department at the University of Pennsylvania. Everything appeared to be going smoothly since he had also found a house for the family in Swarthmore, a suburb of Philadelphia. Arrangements were made with a moving van to move them from Bemus Point, 436 miles away, to their new home.

Moving Turmoil

On September 5th, the moving van arrived at 6 p.m. and loaded up their furnishings. It left shortly after 8 p.m. Two vehicles started the trip: one with Celina, William, and the three children in their old Essex and another with William's mother Louisa, driving with two Indian boys, Wilfred and Anges.

Two miles down the road a car flagged them down and told them the moving van owner could not make the trip for the agreed sum and wanted an additional $15.00. Daddy signed a paper agreeing to pay the additional money by October 10th. The old Essex began sputtering as they traveled through dense fog which had enveloped them. A decision was made to pull off the highway and wait until morning when the fog would clear up.

They reached Harrisburg at 6 p.m. the following day and traveled until the generator on the old Essex refused to supply sufficient electricity to supply the motor and the lights, and went dead. William settled the children with his wife and mother at a roadside camp, attempting to make them comfortable.

He decided to go ahead in his mother's vehicle along with the two Indian boys for the remaining 93 miles to Swarthmore. They arrived at 2 a.m. and found the men in the moving van asleep. They had arrived at 11 p.m. and placed all the furniture onto the veranda and then went to sleep in the van.

William awakened the movers and together they carried everything inside and placed furniture and boxes where they thought items should be placed. After drinking a cup of coffee, they slept until later in the morning.

My father and the boys started back in the afternoon to where the family spent the night figuring the Essex would run in the light of day without problems. Upon arriving, he was thankful his family had passed the night without incident.

They all left for Swarthmore after a late start, but soon they were once again overtaken by darkness and forced to drive up to a farmhouse and leave the Essex behind.

All of them crowded into his mother's car and finished the last fifty miles of their move, finally reaching their destination on the evening of the 7th at 10 pm.

They were greeted by their landlady, Mrs. Sellers the next morning who told them they could not stay because she did not know that my mother was expecting a new addition to the family (that would be me).

William learned this devastating news later that day since he had gone back to tow the Essex to their new home. His notation that day states: "We swallowed our chagrin deciding to look for a new residence the next morning, Saturday, September 9, 1933." After looking at several houses, he selected one at 306 Powell Road for $25 a month which turned out to be satisfactory for them for the next two years.

In his summary of the move from Bemus Point, New York, my father wrote in his daily log, "I thought that it was the hardest trip we have ever had. Sweetheart was completely tired out and of the many trips that we have ever taken this was the worst.

If it had not been for two stops that we made; once when I threw a lot of blankets on the ground and made Sweetheart rest for an hour and the other time when I insisted that we put up at a road-side camp, I feel certain that something (bad) might have happened. The fog, the van owner, the Essex car, the long trip through the night, the lack of sleep - were all harassment.

On top of that, I had forgotten the key to the Essex and had to drive back thirty miles to get it; then had to tow the car. I cringe when I think about the false sense of relief I had when we at finally arrived only to be told we could not stay and would have to move after we had all the furniture set up and in its proper place. Could a trip have had more difficulties?"

My father was a very patient, calm man, indeed. I can imagine I would be a raving lunatic if I had been in that predicament. My mother learned to "roll with the punches," and together they were flexible in adjusting to life's adversities.

They rested for a few days and then moved to 306 Powell Road, Springfield, Pa. on Wednesday, September 13th – home at last! They found the house conveniently located one block from Springfield Central School where my brothers, David, Frederick and sister, Dorothy entered classes. Public transportation, close by in the neighborhood, made it easy for my father to travel to the University of Pennsylvania.

During the next three weeks, he searched for speaking engagements, contacting at least 50 clubs and associations. However, he did not have much luck. Only the Philadelphia Rotary Club gave him a date in November. It seems all clubs and associations were short of money in their budgets for speakers during 1933. Daddy became anxious about finances as his scholarship money wasn't due until October 1st and the $300 they had when they left Bemus Point almost gone. He wondered what they would have done had it not been for Miss Belle Simpson who loaned him $250 before they left Bemus Point which he spent dressing up the family and buying a few other household items. One such expenditure was an amazing electric Easy Washer. This made my mother happy indeed.

My father made a few trips to the University to check out the campus. He found nothing going on until the end of the month when registration would begin. Finally, he met his advisor, Dr. Kelsey, who assisted him in getting registered for Social Institutions, Child Problems, Criminology, Anthropology and Ethnology of America Indians. His instructors were Drs. Kelsey, Bossard, Lichtenberger, Sellin and Speck.

His $830 scholarship money arrived promptly on September 30th, to Daddy's relief. He fervently stated that "no thieving banker" would take his money, since he believed they were not trustworthy. I remember throughout my life seeing my parents keeping careful track of their money and expenses using a ledger. I think they must have kept money under a mattress or in a hidden receptacle. (Years later, I know he became a member of Hillsborough County Credit Union, located in Tampa, Florida.)

My father remarked in his diary on December 2, 1933, that he found the past two months of graduate study very interesting and intensive. He had a little trouble getting back into "form" having been out of college for nine years. His classmates were mostly young men in their twenties but a few were much older than he. He celebrated his 41st birthday on December 17th, thinking the new arrival would come on his birthday, but he was wrong.

About midnight, Dr. Arnold at Ardmore, Pennsylvania, arrived at our abode at 1:18 a.m. and immediately my mother and doctor left for the hospital, arriving at 1:30 am. Eleven minutes later I was born! I am Marilyn Louise Joyce Kasanonkwas Newell. All of us had an Indian name given to us by our parents. A check of my birth certificate tells me that it was not the same way my father spelled it, but I discovered that he had the spelling corrected on December 20th that same year.

My mother and I were doing well at the hospital, but my brothers and sister came down with the chicken pox. Mother told me Dr. Arnold looked in on her quite often during her confinement at the hospital as he knew about the unique circumstances at home, and she fondly remembered his kindness.

A Break in Routine

Christmas vacation started at the University, which made Daddy relieved and happy. Now, he could take care of his children while Mother and I were in the hospital. His mother, Louisa came to help. At the time, the state of her health and her diabetes concerned her. She also thought that my father should contest his father's will because it only gave him $5 with the rest of his property left to his father's wife, Jennie. My father, however, felt that it would be wrong to do so. His father had died on December 1st at age 89 at his home in rural New York. Due to lack of money, he did not travel to New York for the funeral.

My Mother still in the hospital, Daddy undertook the task of cooking a turkey for Christmas dinner. He reported it did not taste as good as when my mother cooked it.

I personally can testify that he did not excel in cooking. Five years later when my sister Diane, was born; Mother in the hospital of course, Daddy cooked our dinner and put nutmeg in our mashed potatoes. They were awful! He reported that the children missed their mother very much, also mentioning that Santa Claus had not been liberal with Christmas presents that year. (1933)

He began work on his Master's thesis: "Crime and Justice Among the Iroquois Nations" which he eventually published. The year ended with his decision to not contest his father's will. It was ten degrees below zero in Philadelphia when my mother and I returned home on December 29th, 1933.

Searching for Opportunities

While my father studied to earn his Master's Degree, he also founded the Neighborhood Indian Society of Philadelphia where Indians participated in social events together, once a month. I found a membership list representing twenty-six tribes; Mohawk and Cherokee predominated. This list, generated on May 17, 1935, showed eighty-four members, thirty-five children, sixteen white wives, two white husbands, and two honorary members for a total of one hundred sixty-two. They also offered assistance to each other in times of need. I have a photo showing my mother holding a teacup with other ladies at a social event, all drinking tea.

He felt honored to receive half tuition in exchange for being a scientific research assistant in Ethnology, Archaeology and Anthropology at The University of Pennsylvania Museum in February 1934. He actually was selected for this opportunity twice, while at the university.

My father graduated with a Master's Degree in Sociology and Anthropology from The University of Pennsylvania in June 1934, exactly ten years after receiving his Bachelor of Arts degree from Syracuse University.

Chapter 7: A Waiting Game to Become a Civil Servant

On August 21, 1934, William took a Civil Service exam in hopes it might help him obtain a position as Supervisor Community Worker with the United States Indian Service at a yearly salary of $3,800. He passed the examination with 'flying colors' learning he had the highest score among several thousand who took the examination. One might say he became "number one" on the list of applicants.

He received letters from his senator and congressman informing him that his prospects of obtaining a position, were very good. In May 1935, he was offered a position at Haskell Institute in Kansas, but for only $2,600. Not what he expected. Time dragged on before he obtained that actual appointment, on August 1, 1935, nearly a year from the time he had taken the exam.

His diary reveals the anguish he experienced during that summer, waiting for news from Washington. On June 11, 1935, he attended the National Conference of Social Work, in Montreal, Canada.

William had been invited to speak on "The Indian Community." The Montreal Star and Montreal Gazette both printed some statements from his speech that the Office of Indian Affairs apparently did not like. So, officials kept him in suspense, and it became a waiting game.

Throughout July he kept waiting for word from Washington – thinking that it would arrive any day. His journal informs us that he had the family "all packed and ready to leave within 24 hours." He had been told on July

1$^{st.}$ it would be a matter of two to ten days before they would leave for Lawrence, Kansas and Haskell Institute. On July 15th, he decided to call a moving van and have their belongings transported to a storage facility. So, this became the beginning of my father's frustrated dealings in the political arena of the Indian Service of the United States. I'd say they did not improve as time progressed.

The 2nd annual picnic of the Society of Neighborhood Indians took place July 20th and the Newell family attended as guests while they waited for their train tickets to arrive and the long journey to begin.

Pursuing New Activities While Waiting

While he waited for a job with the United States Indian Service, he became director of Recreational Activities in Delaware County, Pennsylvania. He organized the following activities: Senior and Junior Orchestras, Singing Classes, Public Speaking Classes, Drama Group, Garden Club, Playground Hour and Amateur Night. Actual payment for these services were often received late and not a dependable source of income.

He continued with numerous speaking engagements in the area. William also continued taking more credits at the University towards a doctorate. He worried endlessly about finances causing him undue anxiety.

At last, they left on an arduous train trip to Lawrence, Kansas, on a hot stuffy day at the end of July. Friends saw them off at the Baltimore and Ohio Railway Station in Philadelphia. They arrived two days later. William took his oath of office, noting "I am now a government employee for the sum of $2,600 per year."

His duties at Haskell Institute, America's largest Indian boarding school, were to teach Community Leadership to twenty specially selected native high school graduates from various high schools throughout the United States. This included teens from Indian reservations. When Washington officials discovered that most of those enrolled, were from cities and only three came from a reservation, his position was abolished a year later.

While at Haskell School he taught this group of 20 students General Anthropology, Ethnology and Community Leadership. At the first faculty meeting in August, the administration asked him to also teach General Anthropology to 30 seniors and to 49 students in Mr. Johnson's commercial group. He believed that they were asking too much for his meager salary of $2,600 per annum, but he persevered.

School started September 9th with a full schedule of classes. Photos in the family album show him with his students with some of them holding models of homo sapiens used in their Anthropology class.

When he had been on the job for one month, he commented that everything is fine except for living quarters: an apartment. "Today the stone courtyard sewer clogged up and we had two inches of water inside our apartment." He continued, "Perhaps the bugs have been washed out so it may not be as bad as it seems." I believe my mother must have been appalled by this event.

He soon received an invitation to teach ethnology at Kansas University from Dr. Carroll Clark, and he hoped that would occur the next term. He had discovered with the change in administration in Washington, his current position would be abolished. In the meantime, he traveled to Kansas City, Missouri to meet officials at the Museum and Council on Social Agencies. There he purchased $200 of Indian artifacts for his own collection.

The following April he received a letter from the Philadelphia Neighborhood Indian Society informing him that he had been elected Honorary President. Also, the Montreal Herald published an article regarding the Canadian Indians asking that he be appointed to the position of "Commissioner of Indian Affairs." This did not

54

happen and someone else filled the position. My father later remarked he would have been elated had he been appointed so he must have been disappointed about that turn of events.

Washington officials sent him a letter on June 18, advising him that the Community Leadership Course would be discontinued and offered him a position as Senior Boys Advisor, Acting Principal and teacher at Wahpeton Indian School in Wahpeton, North Dakota. He accepted. Teaching as an adjunct professor at Kansas University would not have produced enough income. Therefore, in the fall of 1936 our family moved to the state of North Dakota. He regretfully sent a letter to Dr. Clark informing him of his new circumstances. It was a disappointment for them both.

He found himself on horseback for a Fourth of July parade, in buckskin and headdress that summer, and before moving, he did community work with the Potawatomi Indians north of Topeka, Kansas. He had assisted them in organizing recreational activities, called the Big Soldier Playground project. At one of their events there were at least 800 Indians present. Many came from nearby Kickapoo Reservation. The superintendent told him he made their summer recreation program a "howling success," and applauded his efforts telling him "he might get himself adopted into the Potawatomi tribe." Just for the reader's information the Potawatomi were originally from the North East, but their homelands were snapped up by whites after

American Independence and they migrated across the Mississippi and onto reservations in Oklahoma and Kansas.

During 1937 he was also a delegate and speaker at the Institute on Recreational Activities at Washburn College in Topeka, Kansas.

Chapter 8: Achievement Beyond Civil Service

My father transferred to Wahpeton, North Dakota where he began duties as Senior Boys Advisor, teacher and acting principal at Wahpeton Indian School. He continued to be involved in the recreational activities of the children he taught. Photo album snapshots reveal an ice skating rink that he constructed on the school grounds so youngsters would have a fun activity after school.

While there, during 1937 the school changed from a senior to a junior school and this made his position invalid. His services were no longer required. William declared in his writings that it had become a popular opinion held by many individuals at the time that securing a government job was "all that any man would ever want in life." He, however, in 1937 became quite disillusioned with the Civil Service. He wrote, "After the many difficulties my wife and I and our four children have experienced we managed to return east to Philadelphia. It cost me $500 to get out West and then back East, so my two years with the Indian Service were a complete financial loss!" So much for a secure and well-paying position with the Federal Government, for an Indian!

Before traveling back East, he continued with speaking engagements at Capital City Commercial College and Rotary Club in Des- Moines, Iowa. He lectured before the Indianapolis Rotary Club and handled the State Marble

Tournament in Grand Forks, North Dakota for the Knights of Columbus. The Rochester Neighborhood Indian Society (Rochester, New York) made him an Honorary Life Member. Also, that year, the National Research Council, Washington, D.C., added him to in the International Directory of Prehistoric Archaeologists and Anthropologists.

He received a letter from the Bureau of Indian Affairs on December 20^{th,} telling him his highly specialized training made it difficult to find a proper position for him in the Indian Service. This left him with no prospect for a decent job with them. He wrote to a Judge Martin, saying, "I am not at all interested in securing a position in the Indian Service because I have seen too much political cut-throat politics played by the members of this service and it is difficult for them to accept a man of Indian blood with too many college degrees. I am not the first Indian to be shunted out of the service by that gang who has held positions in the Indian Service for many years. I could mention the names of a great many Indians who have tried to survive. . . usually the only ones who do are men with ordinary training."

He continued to lament in his diary, "Upon my return from the West and my disgusting experiences with the government work, I secured a temporary position as docent authority on American Indian Art at the Brooklyn Museum. This happened with the help of Mr. Jayne, assistant director of The Metropolitan Museum of Art in New York City. This became possible because my friend, Mr. Phil Youtz, had to resign from directorship in order for him to accept a position as Director of Art for the Pan American Exposition in California." He expected this position to last for six months.

My father had resigned himself to working in any position among the public rather than as a "specialist" among Indians. He knew about the experiences of others who appeared to succeed when they were working as ordinary citizens. Upon the suggestion that he try to sell bonds to the Indians throughout the West, he wrote in his ledger, "I think I could sell a great many more bonds and stamps to others, but I just don't feel a bit interested in working for any government group that has Indians under their charge."

He resumed, "I am a good speaker, and I have had considerable selling experience having at one time been star salesman for The Magnuson Products Corporation of Brooklyn. If the stock market crash hadn't wrecked this work, I would be in plenty of money. But, I can sell, and I am willing to do so to any group other than Indians. As a matter of fact, I think my own people would rather listen to a white salesman than to one of their own."

He expounded in his diary about The Museum of the American Indian in New York City, "The Heye Foundation at 175th and Broadway has the poorest management in the world. What they need is someone who can make it a real live museum and not a junk shop, such as it is now. They have one of the greatest collections of Indian relics in the world. I might also mention that this institution has such a high quantity of Indian relics that they store most of it up in the Bronx. The New York Daily News severely criticized its director last year for having a bunch of dead museums, particularly, this institution. I don't know the setup or just what can be done to organize and staff it, however."

It seems that George Heye and his brother started this museum and then the brother with the real financial backing died without making provision in his will for the support of the institution. George Heye was old and the museum barely existed with a slim staff.

My father thought this information should be held in confidence since he did not want individuals to think he had anything to do with promoting changes. It wasn't until the 1980's, many years later discussions began with the Smithsonian regarding transferring the museum to them.

In November 1989, President George H. W. Bush signed legislation, creating the National Museum of the American Indian as part of the Smithsonian.

In 1994, George Gustav Heye Center opened in the old Alexander Hamilton Customs House in New York City. The building, originally completed in 1907 covered three city blocks. However, as time progressed, in 1999, a state of the art center was constructed in Suitland, Maryland. From 1994 to 2004, more than 800,000 objects were transferred from the National Museum of the American Indian Research Branch in the Bronx, New York to the new Cultural Resources center.

On September 21, 2004, the National Museum of the American Indian opened on the National Mall in Washington, D.C, with the largest gathering of Native American Communities in history. I feel certain that my father was there in spirit.

Brooklyn to Long Island

During 1938 and 1939 my father gave numerous lectures at public schools while connected with the Brooklyn Museum. He began a ten year association with the prestigious Pratt Art Institute, traveling quite often to give his talks. He used many of the lantern slides he had made which demonstrated the art, utensils, inventions, abodes, food and history of the North and South American Indians.

He describes receiving an extraordinary letter from a principal of Brooklyn Technical High School stating he had never heard such thunderous applause after my father's lecture to some six thousand students (3,000 in the morning and 3,000 in the afternoon). My father commented, "It gave me a wonderful feeling" knowing I had touched so many individuals.

While lecturing at schools, Rotary and Kiwanis clubs, and Mason Lodges, he moved our family from Brooklyn, New York down Long Island to South Hampton, New York in 1938.

By June 1939, he had fulfilled a year's residency including rigid requirements of passing a satisfactory examination before the committee on Christian Education in order to be licensed to preach the gospel.

The chairman of the Examining Committee, Rev. P.E. Radford of Mattituck spoke highly on the excellent results of my father's examination, mentioning he had had no other candidate who presented such a splendid showing of his divinity studies. On June 13th, before the pastors and elders of all the Presbyterian Churches of the Long Island Presbytery, he was confirmed in this sacred rite. My father became a guest minister at various churches and ministered to the Shinnecock Indians who resided close to South Hampton.

As a sociologist he performed a study of the miscegenation of the Shinnecock Indians of Long Island, completing a document which traces the mixture of races through marriage/cohabitation between a white person and a member of another race, black slaves included.

Historians have written about the scattered groups of Native Americans who were decimated by the English and Dutch who had brought death and disease to them. Many left Long Island. A great exodus of natives occurred due to the wars with the colonists. They integrated with other tribes, often moving further into the interior of the United States and Canada.

Native Americans struggled to become recognized as equal citizens in the United States; just surviving was an accomplishment. Many remained on reservations that were diminishing in size and self-sufficiency. While intermarrying with other groups to include whites, they none-the-less lost some of their distinctly Indian ways.

It wasn't until 1924 that Indians were declared U.S. citizens and granted the right to vote. Those in Virginia and in many other states were prevented from going to the polls for years. Not until after World War II did the Federal government insist that Indians, who had been subject to the draft during the war like other citizens, be allowed to vote in Presidential elections. That privilege was not extended to Indians in Maine until 1954.

Chapter 9: A Museum of His Own

William was being encouraged to open his own museum by his colleagues in 1938 with the relics he had collected and with objects on loan from other museums. Our family had moved into a large two storied frame house in a mostly agricultural area north of South Hampton, near the village of Water Mill. The property surrounded by fields of corn, cucumber and potato sat on a main highway.

"Long Island Express"

Before the museum could be realized, the Great Hurricane of 1938 struck Long Island with a vengeance. It held those plans in abeyance. This storm devastated the forests and farms of New England, even creating the Shinnecock Inlet and widened the Moriches Inlet, near South Hampton with its powerful storm surge.

It struck September 21st and is known as one of the deadliest and most destructive tropical cyclones ever to strike this area. Meteorologists monitored its path with the use of barometers and information from ships at sea only. There were no weather satellites, no weather radar and no offshore weather buoys at that time. Instead of curving out to sea as some thought, it picked up forward speed, accelerating to 70 miles per hour (the fastest known forward speed recorded). People really had no warning of the impending danger and the twenty foot storm surge that pummeled the 1000 miles of the New England shoreline.

Statistics reveal that there were 700 deaths recorded, an estimated 2 billion trees lost, and many towns were inundated with water by the storm surge up and down the New England coast. On a positive economic note, it ended the unemployment experienced near the end of The Great Depression. At that time, most people who were out of work would gladly work for the standard wage of $2 per day. Because so much damage had occurred to homes and buildings and so many trees blocked roadways, thousands of people flocked to Long Island in search of clean-up work and repair. In fact more than 2,700 men were brought into New York and New England by Bell Systems just to repair downed phone lines.

The Shinnecock Indians lost their Presbyterian Church located on the eastern side of the Shinnecock Bay. It was torn off its foundation and badly damaged. There were 34 fatalities on Long Island. The population of less than 200 required massive assistance and organizational effort to garner funds to build a new church. Local parishioners mobilized the entire religious community of Suffolk County that included Episcopalian, Presbyterian, Congregational and others to gather funds. The damaged church was salvaged and then used as a community center. A pow-wow held at the reservation in 1938, helped raise funds, and a newly constructed Shinnecock church opened in September 1939.

I have memories of my father leading me out of our home down trembling stairs to a safer location. My brothers and sister were at school, and my mother watched flying debris pass by her hospital window. She had given birth to my sister, Diane Marie Newell, the fifth Newell child on September 11th.

After things returned to normal, my father transformed the house and property to become our American Indian Museum of Arts and Science. The actual museum consisted of three rooms on the ground floor, with the remainder of the house being our living quarters.

Since the sport of lacrosse was invented and played by Indians, my father had a natural love for the sport and therefore laid out a court on our front lawn. That game played by our ancestors is now a popular sport on college campuses. My father reported on this when he worked as a reporter in Syracuse, New York during his undergraduate days. Occasionally, my brothers would demonstrate the sport to interested visitors. This was at a time they were attending South Hampton High School.

My father created a simulated burial rack which displayed how Indians would lay the dead high above the ground so animals would not get at the wrapped body. He also built a work travois consisting of two long poles latched to an animal skin which held goods that could be transported when they traveled. These were placed on the side yard. Tourists enjoyed taking snapshots around these exhibits. (Author in photo)

My mother's contribution consisted of sewing four canvas tee-pees on her sewing machine which stood magnificently in our backyard. I remember her telling me she broke many needles while sewing on that thick canvas material to get that accomplished. A girl-scout troop once camped overnight in them. I personally watched them through my upstairs bedroom window with my nose

65

pressed to the window screen. I was enthralled watching them as they set up camp around the tee-pees. It looked like something I wanted to do, but I thought that it probably wasn't possible since I was only seven years old.

Our Indian Museum opened in June 1940. Large letters were hung in a hedge along one side of the property, which spelled out **I-N-D-I-A-N M-U-S-E-U-M. This** enabled the public traveling down the highway that fronted our house to notice the facility. This proved to be an exciting adventure for our family.

At a benefit event, 103 tickets were sold for an illustrated lecture my father gave. It helped him buy a license for his vehicle which cost $24.75. He still did much traveling to speak to audiences large and small while keeping the museum open throughout the summer into fall. By the end of July attendance reached 888; by August 31, 1,385 tourists paid admission to visit our museum.

The actual museum consisted of three rooms on the ground floor, with the remainder of the house, our living quarters. Whenever I heard a car pull up in the driveway, I knew my father would leave his study where he spent a good deal of time doing research, writing letters on his typewriter and then go to greet the tourists and escort them through the museum. Sometimes, I would tag along, the wooden floors creaking as we walked from room to room. My favorite part came when he removed real Amazon shrunken heads from their protective case. Even though I shivered, they were quite intriguing. They looked sad with frowns on their faces, rightfully so.

My mother decided to have Indian baskets and jewelry available to visitors at the end of their tour should they want an authentic souvenir. When we closed the museum for the season in early November, that year, Daddy recorded 2,658 adults, and 248 children had paid admission to visit our museum. He reported he earned an additional $345 for lectures he gave that year also. (Photo: William, Celina, Dorothy and Joyce Newell, 1942)

Chapter 10: Aiding World War II Effort

The Museum opened its second year on May 1, 1941 with attendance on the upswing with a total attendance of 2,899 by the end of September. My brother, Bill graduated from South Hampton High School. His graduating class, numbering 77, attended our museum along with the principal, Mr. Sabine in May.

An Exciting Night with Bill Newell

Bill had taught himself to play the trumpet and with his friend, Billy, a jazz pianist, they looked for places where they might get the opportunity to perform. They found a highly touted jazz spot, The Bluebird, in nearby Riverhead. On numerous occasions they talked about experienced black musicians, awaiting a gig close to New York City allowing them to sit-in as performers on stage.

It happened one night that my brother Bill and his musician buddy had a very profound experience while returning from a gig at the Bluebird. The only reason I know is because I uncovered a story he had written late in his life about how he helped capture German spies.

History tells us that in 1942, Nazi German U-boat attacks officially began against merchant ships along the eastern seaboard of North America. They continued in "Operation Drumbeat" for seven months sinking fuel tankers and cargo ships with impunity, and often within sight of shore. They destroyed 233 ships in the Atlantic Ocean and Gulf of Mexico killing 5000 seamen and passengers. The US Navy lied to the public about the terrifying U-Boat attacks.

Traveling home one night, they noticed a vehicle that did not have their headlights partially covered as mandated by the government. At the time there was a special blackout ordered for all Long Island because the lights from homes and cars on the highways threw up a glare that silhouetted the merchant vessels as they traveled along the coast of Long Island. These ships were "sitting ducks" for German subs. They weren't as easy to spot without the glare, therefore, cars had to have ¾ of their headlights taped for nighttime driving.

Together, my brother and his fellow musician mustered up enough courage to get this vehicle to stop so they could inform its driver about the restriction. The driver flashed an identification card and said menacingly, "Lt.Stump, F.B.I. Now, move along," in an unmistakable German accent. The card looked legitimate and had his picture on it. He and Billy fired back with a "Yes, sir," and added, "Sorry Lieutenant."

This was only the beginning of their adventure that scary night, as their suspicion ignited and they decided to switch off their own headlights and follow the car they had stopped. Adrenalin kept them going as they had a difficult time maneuvering their car to stay on the roadway and not go off into a ditch. When the car they were following turned off the main road, it stopped a short time later and the driver got out at a house. The two teens watched from a safe distance. Gathering up their gumption, the two 17 year old boys snuck up and wrote down the car's tag number and the house number; made a careful U-turn on the darkened road and high tailed it toward South Hampton. They did not turn on their headlights until they saw a car approaching in the distance.

They drove straight to the South Hampton Police Station and reported their news. The police then telephoned the New York City F.B.I. office and soon agent, P. E. Foxworth was on the line questioning them.

Headlines in the New York papers a short time afterwards confirmed that he and his fellow musician had indeed aided the war effort: "German Spies Land on Long Island; FBI seizes 8." The article continued: Saboteurs from German U-Boat rounded up on the beach near Montauk, Long Island. Agent, P.E. Foxworth led the G-Men in the capture.

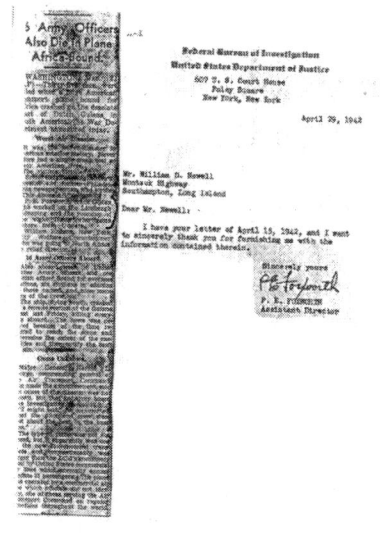

I found this story written by my brother fascinating and made me swell with pride at his bravado because he actually had contact with one of them – confronting an agent on a dark road because his headlights were not partially covered. These two brave boys had an exciting night that "showed their courage and patriotism." They were responsible for instigating an investigation that resulted in the capture of eight German spies. My parents also were overjoyed about Bill's adventure and the resulting capture. My brother received a letter from the F.B.I thanking him for the information that enabled them to proceed with their investigation.

War Engulfs the United States

Meanwhile, on the world stage, the United States had declared war against Japan after their ferocious attack at Pearl Harbor on December 7, 1941. We also entered the war against Nazi Germany who had a ruthless leader, Hitler, intent on capturing nation after nation in Europe, with his maniacal ambitions. It appeared many of the world's nations were engulfed in The Great World War II. However, history reveals that a few countries somehow managed to remain neutral.

Our Native American Museum of Arts and Science opened for a third season on April 2, 1942. It appeared on all Long Island maps for the year 1942 as a special point of interest, but due to gasoline rationing, attendance began to fall. My father continued with his speaking engagements in the area informing his audiences how fortunate they were to be within an easy driving distance to the museum. He explained that our institution depended to a great extent on the traveling public for attendance.

While this statement could be true of any museum in any city; he feared our museum would suffer from the restrictions on tourist travel and depend even more on local support.

Chapter 11: Working Again for Civil Service

The museum closed the end of October that year 1942, with attendance only at a meager 871 visitors. At that point, my father began to work for the War Department as chief clerk at Montauk Point (Long Island), New York. Listed in his diary is the fact that during this time as a confidential secretary to Ordinance officer for the harbor defenses of Long Island Sound he received a commendation from First Service Command for suggestions he made which aided the war effort.

My younger brother, Louis became eager to join the U.S. Marines and persuaded my father to sign for him; not being 18 years old.

Life at Fort H.G. Wright Army Base, Fisher's Island, N.Y.

On April 3, 1944, our museum closed its doors permanently and stored its possessions. My father then transferred to Fort H.G. Wright Army Base, located on Fisher's Island where we lived for the remainder of the war.

This island is two miles off the coast of Connecticut and is nine miles long and one mile wide. (Today it is a popular destination for summer travelers and wealthy elite residents such as Oprah Winfrey.) In 1944, the army base occupied only a small portion of the island, with the remainder, private properties. Ferry service ran twice daily between the island and New London, Connecticut.

My father had worked with the Civil Service in various positions which included firefighter with the rank of captain. He still traveled to give lectures for Pratt Institute and the Brooklyn Institute of Arts and Sciences. He mentions that his car mileage for the month of January was 1,868 miles and that he had spent $78.80 on the engine repairs. This must have been what prompted him to decide to stop driving and announce that he sold his vehicle for the sum of $100. On February 17th 1945, he announced that it would be his last day for driving a car. After that date he either walked or took public transportation wherever he or members of our family traveled. I remember always taking a bus downtown and walking everywhere.

He traveled to Norwich, Connecticut to arrange for lectures at the University of Connecticut, stopping at Connecticut State Teacher's College in Connecticut as well. When November came, my father observed that he had accumulated five years in the Civil Service.

1946

January 1946 began with both of my parents "under the weather." My mother wrenched her back lifting a 14-quart pail of water from the washing machine into the sink and suffered from pain for three weeks. Neither the 500-watt heat lamp nor three applications of Grandpa's salve gave her much relief. My father suffered from bronchitis and the post doctor ordered him to bed for a couple of days. His illness lasted for ten days before he returned to work and he still felt poorly. He remarked that he is having sinus headaches and prescribed drops did not ease the pain.

On the home front, we were informed that my brother, Bill, then enrolled at Northwestern University, near

Chicago, Illinois married fellow student Carol Miller. My older sister, Dorothy began violin lessons and I began piano lessons. We traveled by ferry to New London, Connecticut occasionally for shopping, and supplies about an hour's travel time, while we lived on the army base. Our living quarters, government housing, referred to as the "Blue Tops," were white houses with blue metal roofs. We lived high up on a bluff not far from the women's barracks, overlooking Long Island Sound. Our entertainment consisted of attending movies at the base theater and occasionally we went to the bowling alley. We bought our groceries from the base post-exchange. Neighborhood kids played hide and seek among the sandbagged gun embankments, overlooking the ocean.

This author is reluctant to imagine what might have occurred in our corner of the universe had any military action taken place in the U-Boat infested waters around us. I was oblivious to the dangers as a 12 year girl.

My brother, Louis came home on leave for a week the end of February, returning to his base located in Richmond, Virginia on March 10th, 1946. When he was discharged in May, my father declared he "got a bad deal from the government and the Marines, and thanked God that he is over with it."

Life in the Fire Department

Internal politics were rampant in the fire department on base between the chief and other firefighters, including my father. My father's diaries continually reported disputes. Once an employee blamed him for a difficult Fire Fighting course of training that they had to endure that was given by Chief Leonard. He claimed the chief was trying to show that he knew more than my father about technical Fire Fighting. My father remarked that he had never given a thought that there might have been a feud between them, as suggested by this employee. Much later he decided there may have been something to that idea.

In April, he took an automobile road test and failed to pass for a driver's permit, and Chief Leonard threatened to demote one pay grade to all who failed to pass it. My father announced that working for the government can be very depressing – thinking that if Leonard would be truthful about events, things would not be so bad. He said he never knew whose side Leonard favored or just what his actions would be. Ten days later, on April 16th, two employees were given notice and it looked like there would be a shifting around of employees with a few coming over from Montauk Point.

World War II ended on September 2, 1945 and a rumor spread that the Fire Department would be closed, therefore my father began recruiting at Universities and Colleges for a teaching position. He mailed 300 letters that he had mimeographed applying for a sociology teaching job. He received a few negative responses, but did not get depressed. Instead he persevered in his efforts. Like Buddha, he became impervious to suffering. He confronted his life challenges with inner strength and courage.

Chapter 12: A Rewarding Life as Professor Newell

His diligent efforts paid off. On July 23rd, my father personally met with University of Connecticut school officials, Dr. Burroughs, Dr. Hypes, Dr. Barnett and Dr. Knoblauch who offered him a teaching job at the New London branch teaching Sociology and Anthropology. At last, he would be doing what he knew best, teaching; not just high school pupils, but adults in a university setting. This was excellent news, as this was the career for which he was destined. It buoyed his spirit.

At this point, my father looked for housing for our family in New London, Connecticut in August, locating an appropriate house at 27 Alger Place, in a middle-class neighborhood. We moved there on September 2, 1946. He recorded that the fire department would be abolished on October 1, 1946. At last things were looking up. His life was evolving in a better direction.

He had accumulated five years with the War Department, two of which were with the fire department on an army base. He struggled, but he had survived those 24 months of grueling frustration. He felt tremendous relief to be free of its inner politics and tumultuous atmosphere. While there he experienced a high stress level. There were six legal sized typewritten pages of his diary devoted to daily exploits within the department during 1946.

My father had two weeks of leave accrued and left Fort H.G. Wright Army Base to pursue his new life as a university professor. He helped register students on September 21st at the New London branch of the University of Connecticut. He set up his office on campus, which had a good location for his extensive book collection.

My older sister, Dorothy began work working at the University. My brother Louis began work at Lawrence Memorial Hospital. My brother Bill and wife, Carol came from Chicago looking for work on October 1st. I began 7th grade at Harbor School and received my first pair of roller skates. Life was good.

We entertained relatives who visited us from Montreal in September and Daddy gave an illustrated lecture at the University auditorium for the 175 students enrolled in his Sociology and Anthropology classes, in November. He remarks that he had been quite occupied with his classes and did not have time to write in his diary.

Uplifted in Spirit in 1947

My extended family was united at Christmas that year and Daddy happy and satisfied with life in general. We all had smiles in a picture taken in the living room that I found in a scrapbook. One day, he brought home an alley cat that hung around the New London branch of the University and it ate lettuce and water instead of milk and meat. We named the cat Me-Too. It also ran up and down the keyboard of our piano in the middle of the night, "Me-too" must have inspired my father, as he surprised me one day when I heard him banging out "Oh Susanna" on the piano. My thought is that he had learned something about music at that convent where he had resided as a lad as it seemed he could easily play this tune and others.

A New England style house with its bay window and porch became our home for the next two years. It had a heavenly scented lavender lilac tree along with a lovely pear tree in the backyard, and Lily of the Valley blooming under the hedge. It came furnished with beautiful mahogany dining and living room furniture, which I dusted as one of my chores. Lace curtains decorated the windows. I enjoyed my years there in that comfortable home.

My parents either went to the movies or to bingo games at the local churches for their entertainment. My father meticulously recorded their winnings but mostly losses in his records. They did not appear to be significant at all. Gambling just was not that exciting, especially when your losses exceed your winnings. Gambling never appealed to me either.

We traveled to Gainesville, Florida for the summers of 1947 and 1948 where Daddy became Associate Professor of Sociology at the University of Florida. Our family had happy days there in Gainesville, for those two summers. My father enrolled me for swimming lessons at the university pool with football players who towered over me. I found it a little unnerving - a shy girl of 14, but I survived that ordeal, and did learn to swim. We traveled as a family by Greyhound bus both times to that destination. Both my sister Diane and I were somewhat traumatized by motion sickness on those trips. I have good memories of my parents and me walking to downtown Gainesville to events on the Square and of attending movies with them. It was about a one mile walk from the lovely home we rented from one of the professors. On the way home a stop at the bakery was an important one. One day my father asked the clerk "What's on those buns – honey?" To which she replied in her southern drawl, "Cinnamon and pecans." We laughed about that for years afterwards. My father remained the Chairman of the Department of Sociology at the Trumbull Branch of the University of Connecticut during those years as well.

Upon my graduation from Harbor School eighth grade in 1948 we ended up moving to Tampa at the end of the summer term in Gainesville. My mother had decided she wanted to leave the cold winters of the north behind and my father agreed. This rather abrupt move in August, 1948, began our residency in the hot humid climate of Tampa, Florida where we were to remain for many years.

Chapter 13: National Recognition and Move to Tampa

The year 1948 was a very memorable year for all of us. My father had an extensive listing in Who's Who in American Education, Who's Who in New England, followed by a listing in Who's Who in America (1950, 1952, 1964-65) and Who's Who in the South, 1950. He also became listed in the International Directory of Prehistoric Archaeologists & Anthropologists. He had certainly earned these prestigious recognitions.

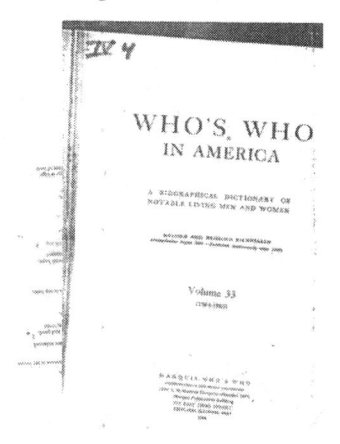

My father had returned north to dispose of the belongings of our house at 27 Alger Place and we started over in Tampa, living in a rented dwelling on South Street in Seminole Heights. There were four of us living there. My sister, Diane, myself and Mother and Father were all that came to Tampa. He found work with the Hillsborough County Board of Public Instruction as a teacher at Mango Elementary School for two years. He transferred later to Brandon High School where he remained until retirement in June 1959. That was a huge change from the teaching of university students to that of young pupils. He just wanted to keep his Sweetheart happy. He was then, 56 years old.

Since my father did not own an automobile nor drive any longer, he had to arrange for someone to transport him to Mango Elementary School and then later to Brandon High School from our West Tampa address. I took two city buses to get to Hillsborough High School where I attended 1950 through 1952.

Daddy, a teacher and advisor for the Brandon High newspaper, The Eagle's Eye, led his students to win 16 national awards for excellence. More honors followed in the school year 1954-55 when it was the recipient of National First Place award by the Columbia Scholastic Press Association.

My mother always seemed to be enthralled with Florida and viewing orange and grapefruit trees growing on many properties near our house. As a family, we traveled to Florida's tourist attractions including Ross Allen's Silver Springs where we rode the glass bottom boats and watched Allen milking rattlesnake's venom. We were enthralled with Cypress Gardens and their impressive water-ski show and that of Weeki Wachee Springs and the mermaid show.

William Newell with Brandon High School students, 1956

Chapter 14: The Big "C" and Blindness

I graduated from Hillsborough High School in 1952 and entered the University of Tampa that fall semester. Sometime during 1953, my father, who had been a heavy smoker for many years became affected with a nagging sore throat and hoarseness which he thought was the end of a cold.

After three weeks, he continued experiencing difficulty swallowing and coughing. His physician recommended that he travel to John Hopkins Medical Center in Baltimore, Maryland where he could be further analyzed. This he did.

The results revealed that he had laryngeal cancer. In my research, I discovered that it is the 2nd most common site for head and neck malignancy. In the United States alone 11,000 cases are reported annually, usually appearing in males and has a peak incidence during the sixth and seventh decades of life; this according to Medscape website.

Daddy was 61 years old when he had a partial Laryngectomy performed in Tampa at St. Joseph's Hospital. I remember a long scar on his neck which went from one ear to his other ear. The only details I have regarding his recovery are that he had a tracheostomy and had the assistance of a speech therapist to help him to learn how to speak again. Once fully recovered he could talk only in a loud whisper. This, however, did not dampen his enthusiasm for life.

I recall the lyrics of a song my father enjoyed called the "Bluebird of Happiness." It is sung by baritone singer, Jan Pierce. It became a favorite of his. It relates that we all equally experience good and bad times during our lifetime.

The lyrics tell us the king, the pauper, the actor, and the man -on -the -street are all treated just the same by fate, and it useless to get downhearted, when things go awry. I listened to that song as I wrote this chapter, and it made me realize that he was an optimist, as I am, and although he had many setbacks and disappointments during his lifetime he held fast to the hope he would eventually find that bluebird of happiness.

He continued his life in ways that always surprised us. Daddy substituted lemon drops for cigarettes, and while he recuperated, tried his hand at gardening; planting ten rose bushes in our backyard. Roses are sometimes difficult to manage in the humid Florida climate with troubling "black spot" disease, fungus and other issues associated with growing them. His were magnificent when in bloom and he attributed that to banana peels that he placed around them, which he claimed provided special nutrients.

No Voice Now

He returned to teaching at Brandon High School using a microphone in the classroom for another five years until 1959 when he retired. He was a rank 1 teacher, since he had continued to take courses towards a Ph.D. at various times hoping to attain that degree one day. However, he did not. He was not able to achieve this.

Blindness

A scrap of paper from the family photo album in my father's handwriting documents the timeline of events from

February 1, 1958, stating "starting to go blind in right eye on this date...March 1, 1958, slight haze film, filled with moving filaments in left eye, but no fog...definite fog has developed in right eye...Dr. Haddad confirmed on August 5, 1958...Dr. Parsons operated for cataract on right eye." His eyesight restored, he decided to retire from the rigors of teaching in 1959 at age 66, thinking he would soon be eligible for Social Security if he garnered the required number of "quarters."

He did this by putting in some hours at the small neighborhood convenience store at the end of his street, which he was not the least bit embarrassed to do. Again, he showed everyone that he would do whatever was necessary to achieve his goals.

Like the Lakota author, Joseph M. Marshall, III, my father believed in standing up to life's adversities no matter how many times they try to defeat us. If one remains standing in the storms of life, that is enough. "Being strong means taking one more step toward the top of the hill, no matter how weary you may be," Marshall asserts in his book "Keep Going, The Art of Perseverance."

Relaxing at Last

My father remained productive after retirement by editing the Hillsborough County Teacher newsletter for $1 a year; continuing on his path of journalistic endeavors. He assisted with the organization of a city/county cultural committee which formed the Museum of Science and Natural History. Its physical location was 1101 East River Cove, in Sulpher Springs area of north Tampa. My brother Bill and wife Carol also assisted in this endeavor. I recall one room filled with crystals and rocks that glowed luminously under black lights. My science professor, Clyde Reed from the University of Tampa had assisted in one of the museum displays.

This young museum was backed by many local distinguished citizens. Promoted by the academic community, it became the forerunner of today's prominent Museum of Science and Industry across from the University of South Florida on Fowler Avenue, Tampa, Florida.

Chapter 15: Retirement and European Adventures

Finally retired, my father acquired Social Security, a small pension from the government for his years with the Civil Service and one from the State of Florida for the 11 years of teaching in Hillsborough County, Florida. He may have had a small pension from his years of service as a minister.

My parents decided to visit Canada where they had both resided in childhood to renew ties with relatives and the Caughnawaga Reservation. On October 10, 1962, an article was published in the Montreal Star titled, "Retired University Professor," with a subtitle "Caughnawaga Indian Comes Home."

It summarizes his life's exploits and how he felt like a stranger, returning after many years away, unable to recognize old faces and landmarks. He still retained his identity with the community. However, to the many Indians living there, he was viewed as an outsider who had abandoned the old way of life. He probably felt somewhat alienated but this did not stop him from organizing The Caughnawaga Historical Society, serving as its first president. I am reminded of a philosophy that comes to mind, that my father demonstrated throughout his lifetime.

"Skillful effort has four parts: preventing negative states of mind, overcoming negative states of mind, cultivating positive states of mind, and maintaining positive states of mind."

In June 1963, my father informed Harold Poitras of The Montreal Star that Britain's grand old statesman, Sir Winston Churchill had acknowledged his partial Mohawk ancestry by becoming an honorary charter member of the newly founded Caughnawaga Historical Society.

My father had wanted to do something for the benefit of the Caughnawaga Reservation where he grew up. Quoted in the article he stated "I feel that if the people of my generation do not capture the history of the Indians, it will be forgotten." This is why he founded the organization which then decided to confirm honorary charter membership to Sir Winston Churchill, whose great grandmother was of Iroquois origin.

It was disclosed that Sir Winston's great grandfather traveled widely on the North American Continent and on one occasion was befriended by an Indian maiden of the Mohawk tribe. He apparently promised to return one day and marry her, which he subsequently did.

The British statesman in reply to a letter of nomination written from 28 Hyde Park Gate, London, stated "I am indeed obliged to you for the agreeable compliment which you pay me, and I warmly reciprocate your good wishes. Yours very sincerely, (signed) Winston Churchill."

European Adventures

After visiting relatives in Montreal, my parents left for Europe. In 1963 they sailed on the Netherlands built luxury ocean liner known as "The Grande Dame". First christened by Queen Juliana of the Netherlands in 1958, it sailed from 1959 until her retirement in 2000. My father thought it was time to return to Europe since he had not been back since his deployment in 1918. They visited for an extended period- of- time, settling in the town of Monchengladbach, Germany. My sister, Dorothy and her husband, T/Sgt. Robert B. Wood were stationed at Rheindahlen Royal Airforce Base in the town of Monchengladbach.

Located west of the Rhine River, between Dusseldorf and the Dutch border, it served as "headquarters" for my parents when they visited Europe on two separate vacations. They lived at 405 Monchengladback-Dorfhausen, Flachbleiche Block 116, Flat 1, Germany for the next 13 months, as arranged by their son-in-law.

Daddy was eager to re-visit Paris where he once lived during World War I, and other cities in Europe, as he had a central location from which he could easily travel to Amsterdam, Paris, and Vienna. My mother called Vienna, "the city of my dreams," as she had dreamt of visiting it one day, and now that time had arrived.

Personally, I was happy that they began to enjoy their retirement to the fullest extent, but I no longer have daily logs or diaries to which I can refer for information advising me of their whereabouts as they traveled to points of interest in Europe. As the mother of four children under the age of six years, I did not keep up with their activities abroad.

While my mother and sister, Dorothy and her young daughter, Bonnie Lynn went shopping and did errands, my father became a little bored and wanted to be productive, much the way I am and he decided to start a coin collection. He began visiting local banks and contacting others as far away as Libreville, Gabon, in Western Africa.

In April 1964, the Monchengladbacher Stradpost featured my father in an extended article with the headline: Rolling Thunder Searches for Old Coins. It revealed some of my father's life story thus far and that he was looking for something meaningful to do while he was on an extended holiday there. It told about the recently formed Caughnawaga Historical Society and how they managed to induct Sir Winston Churchill into it as a charter member.

His collection grew as he made daily visits to banks until everybody knew him by his first name. He joined every coin club he could find and wrote letters to others not in the immediate vicinity.

Chapter 16: A Review of "Crime and Punishment"

Upon returning to the states and to Tampa, on September 24, 1964, my parents decided to explore where they might want to reside and proceeded to apply at various retirement communities that included ones located in Lakeland, Tampa, and St. Petersburg. They discovered that they had to apply and be placed on a waiting list. In the meantime, they decided to lease an apartment in downtown St. Petersburg for six weeks.

One extremely hot and humid day, my father became dizzy and collapsed onto the sidewalk while walking to the local bank. He merely stood up, dusted himself off and continued on his errand only later would it be determined that he had suffered from a stroke known as a "transient ischemic attack."

My father, not one to be idle even as he recovered from his stroke, published his Master's thesis from 1934 by McGill University Press. His work, entitled "Crime & Justice Among the Iroquois Nations" ranks as the first historical document about Caughnawaga Indians that was written by an Indian. It was issued by the Caughnawaga Historical Society which he had organized in 1962-1963.

Excerpts from his document as stated in an article written by William Wardwell state "A study of Iroquois culture might point the way to future peace and happiness of the world. If we analyze the present world situation we readily come to the conclusion that European races and their descendants are even as barbarous, cruel and inhuman as they were when America was first discovered." Further revelations are stated: "Their greed for power, riches and control, their lack of appreciation for human life, their mad rush to invent even greater devices to exterminate their brother/man . . . the gradual mental and physical collapse of men, all these illustrate a greater degree of barbarism than the world has known. Modern races are far more bloodthirsty then they were 300 years ago."

My father elaborates further: "More crime exists, more criminals are born every day; the mental capacity of the human race is slowly degenerating. The mad race to nowhere is dangerously near an end."

The American Indians were doing all right until the white men came along to enlighten them. This was the conclusion of my father's revelations after extensive research and reference to dozens of books by other experts.

He further reported, "Evidently, it would seem that between whiskey and Christianity, Indian morals have suffered badly . . . Distortion and inaccuracy have placed sundry atrocities at the doorstep of the Indian, such as burning at the stake and scalping, but, history shows that in fact these were ideas brought over by the Spanish, French and English.

Even the practice of scalping which was supposed to have existed around the St. Lawrence area, was a European innovation brought about by the French during their long journeys to Iroquoian country. The universal custom to bring home the heads of the enemy was too much for French canoes, hence the scalp lock instead of the head," the 90- page book asserts.

At the time white men arrived with new ideas about property and trade, and the use of firewater spawning vagrancy and intemperance; theft was the "most despicable of crimes." While it is true that theft was practically unknown among all Indian groups and that it was so rare that the only punishment was ridicule and derision, the time did come with the advent of the white invasion that the extent and punishment of theft were no longer the same. For instance, the Creek Indians adopted European methods of punishment, varying in degree. For instance, "stealing is punished for the first offense, by whipping; for the second by the loss of the ears; for the third, by death; the amount stolen disregarded."

One crime that concerned the Indians was that of witchcraft. It was punishable by death. One fatal blow from a tomahawk was administered with the consent of the offender's relatives after a tribal council investigation.

Murder

As for murder, which was rare, it was normal for that act to be handled by families. Normally, the nearest relative of the deceased and the tribal council would decide the punishment.

Historian Morgan Lewis reported, "Murder, was punished with death; but the act was open to condonation. Sir William Johnson said, "In cases of murder, the relatives are left to take what revenge they please." Generally they were unwilling to inflict capital punishment, as it defeated their objective to increase their numbers. In times of war nearly all families who lost a relative in battle were willing to accept a captive enemy, by adoption, to replace the lost one.

Murder, if committed under the influence of liquor, was not punished among the Delawares the murderer had to pay a hundred fathoms of wampum for the murder of a man and two hundred for that of a woman. Often, friends helped with this process, if the murderer was too poor to raise that amount. They then turned it over to the relatives of the slain, at the same time delivering an apologetic speech.

If anyone murdered his own relative, he usually escaped punishment as the family could easily find reason for the deed, and did not wish to lose two members at once.

A murderer was bound to suffer mentally all the days of his remaining life if he did not satisfy the customs of his nation. It was rare before the introduction of liquor for an Indian to commit murder. If this serious act was committed by a sober person, and pardoned by the offended family(through acceptance of the ransom belt) as arranged, he would still suffer the consequences of his act. If the victim was held in high esteem by the family and they felt that the departed spirit could not rest, then the death penalty was insisted upon. If, the murder happened in the same family, a price was accepted rather than decrease the numbers of the family, depending on the circumstances surrounding the crime.

Further, my father determined that Indians were not revengeful. He explains that, "more wrongs have been forgiven, forgotten or ignored by the Indian race than any race I know of. The fact that a life was demanded in the case of murder was fulfilled not so much from the desire to actually satisfy any revengeful feelings on the part of any of the kin of the murdered one, nor was it from the desire to inflict punishment on the offender, but rather it was demanded as a way to appease the spirit of the departed one who could not rest until this spiritual or superstitious belief had been complied with."

He continues, "At least the Indian had a reason for taking the life of an individual even though it may have been a superstitious one, but we of the modern age send a man to the chair for no other reason than to punish the man or to satisfy the revengeful feelings of society against a murderer."

More Travels

My parents visited my brother Louis in Houston in 1966, where they attended a baseball game, marveling at the air-conditioned Astrodome. After a short stay, they flew to Montreal for another visit with old friends and relatives before leaving for Europe for another holiday in Germany, in Mochengladbach. They left September 12, 1966; this time their journey lasted eleven months.

Upon returning to the states, my parents lived in various high rise apartments for senior citizens: first in Lakeland and then at Bayshore Presbyterian Apartments on Barcelona Avenue in Tampa.

In 1971, my parents celebrated their 50th Wedding Anniversary at a party in August midst family and friends at Tampa Federal Savings & Loan Association building. My mother posed with her great grandson Tommy, and mother, Susan and daughter, Diane in a "four generations" pose. (Photo: left to right, Bill, Celina, William, Diane, and Joyce Newell)

Not all family members were present. My sister, Dorothy was still located in Germany and my brother, Louis in Houston, Texas.

At the end of their second vacation in Germany, my father assembled his extensive world coin collection and mounted them onto boards which were covered with royal blue satin. It looked impressive.

In the February 12, 1976 edition of The Tampa Tribune, times writer, Marlene Davis wrote an article, "He's A Jack of All Trades" on the front of Section D, Part IV, featuring my father and displaying his coins. The Landmark Bank of Tampa bought his collection and designed the whole bank around it, displaying it in their lobby.

The feature story summarized my father's adventures, challenges, and accomplishments as he traveled through life. Note, at this point in his life he wanted to explore more opportunities to attain fulfillment. He was 84 years old.

Chapter 17: Indian Nations Rise Up

In the fall of 1976, extensive newspaper articles appeared nationwide, telling about allegations of illegal transfers of tribal lands hundreds of years ago. In Maine, a lawsuit filed by the Passamaquoddy and Penobscot nations in 1972 had alleged that the government owed them $300 million for illegal transfers of tribal lands which covered 60% of the state of Maine. The dispute disrupted Maine municipalities and dried-up markets for municipal bonds, threatening to reduce sources of mortgage loans for businesses, farms and homes. Everyone in New England was "up in arms" over the allegations.

It was the largest of several New England lawsuits filed by lawyers and the Native American Rights Fund, an Indian advocacy organization based in Colorado. Other suits were also filed in Rhode Island, Connecticut and Cape Cod.

Maine's chief legal officer, State Attorney, General Joseph E. Brennan, deemed it "preposterous." Nicholas Sappiel, leader of the Penobscot Indians was quoted, "Now, they're getting a few gray hairs." The lawsuit based on the Indian Non-intercourse Act of 1780, ordered that all land dealings with Indian tribes must be approved by Congress. He continued, "They used to laugh about this case and everything else. Now you have never seen so many lawyers. It reminds you of a cartoon, everybody's so mad."

Five years later, in March 1977, the Justice Department mapped out a plan for a negotiated settlement of the claims of two Maine Indian nations. They cut the original 12.5 million acres to 5 million acres, which affected some 90,000 non-Indians.

Three months before President Jimmy Carter left office the Maine Indian Claims Settlement was finally signed in October 1980. Under the law, Passamaquoddy and Penobscot nations agreed to forfeit their land claims in exchange for $81.5 million, which could be used to buy 300,000 acres from nearby landowners.

Secondly, a trust fund for these nations 0f $27 million was set up for economic development. They also achieved federal recognition, which allowed them to control hunting and trapping on all of their lands, fishing on some of their waters and operate tribal courts with powers similar to those tribal courts operated by other federally recognized nations. This settlement is far and away the greatest Indian victory of its kind in the history of the United States.

During the signing ceremony, Carter called the conflict in Maine an "intolerable situation" and the act was one of the "most difficult issues" he faced as president. He continued, "I aroused the animosity and the criticism of almost everyone at least for transient periods of time . . . the courage of all those here to face a difficult issue head-on has resulted in a settlement that is gratifying to everyone involved."

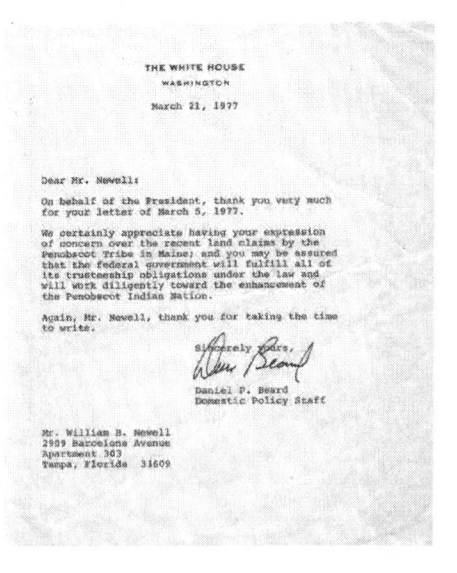

My parents about this time decided to settle down on the Penobscot Old Town Reservation on Indian Island,

Maine. They could not be members of both the Mohawk Nation and the Penobscot Nation as they were long considered adversaries. Keep in mind that my paternal grandmother, Louisa was Mohawk and buried on St. Regis Reservation on the United States side (it is divided by Canada). Remember that my mother, Celina was a Mohawk as well. This meant renouncing their Mohawk association and becoming members of the Penobscot Nation. They secured an apartment in senior housing and settled down. It wasn't long before they discovered that they were both considered outsiders, even though the Newell lineage goes back to include Louis B. Newell aka Rolling Thunder, his own father. They were not heartily welcomed.

My mother managed to acquire a piano for the senior center to add some enjoyment for them, but did not feel appreciated for her efforts. My father purchased a television set for the center as well. The Penobscot residents reacted with aloofness that is still disconcerting. My sister, Diane Wilson Leary lived on the reservation as well along with her husband, Howard and children for several years, without incident.

Chapter 18: National Recognition on Origin of Thanksgiving

At 84, Daddy gained national recognition following his publication of a radically different version of the origin of Thanksgiving as headlined in Bangor Daily News of December 10th, 1977. It read: Professor Gaines Fame for Research, followed by a description of what my father brought to light concerning the feast we name Thanksgiving.

Steve Cartwright, staff writer, interviewed my father who had done his research of colonial records and discovered the festive U.S holiday celebrated the massacre of 700 Pequot Indians in 1637. This had been published in Wabanaki Alliance, a Maine Indian monthly newspaper, and was picked up by the United Press International (UPI) and distributed newspapers.

My father displayed dozens of letters he received from interested persons from California, Washington and Florida. He was interviewed by an Ohio radio station and received a request to appear on television. A number of scholarly inquiries were also received.

My father noted that not one letter or phone call he received was critical of his findings which a University of Connecticut professor stated were based on documents that have been around for years. Not one person disputed what my father called the "true version of the history of Thanksgiving."

Yet, my father was the first scholar to publicize the facts. Briefly, Cartwright elaborates that English and Dutch colonists brutally attacked the Pequots near what is now Groton, Connecticut while the Indians were holding their traditional Green Corn Dance. "700 men, women and children were burned to death in 1637. In commemoration of that deed, the first Thanksgiving Day ever proclaimed in America, was proclaimed by Massachusetts Bay Colony, thanking God that they had dispatched those 700 men, women and children."

The first national Thanksgiving Day wasn't until 1789, when George Washington proclaimed Thursday, November 26, a feast day in honor of a political victory. Apparently, non-Indian Americans have been eating turkey in blissful ignorance of the true origin of the occasion for celebration.

Amherst professor, Dr. Jean E. Ludtke saw the story in the college daily, and wrote to him requesting a list of historical documents for use with his students. My father gladly offered to furnish a list of documents to him and to any others who might be interested. My father never denied that Pilgrims and Indians feasted together. When European settlers first arrived, Indians saved them from starvation and disease and provided them with fresh food. Also, there were many dates in history telling of feast days that were celebrated after fall harvests by both settlers and natives.

Return to Tampa and the End of His Life

My parents returned to Tampa to live at Bayshore Presbyterian Apartments and after a short illness, my father died on January 16, 1981. He was 88 years of age. He is buried on Indian Island, on the Penobscot Nation Reserve. My mother died in January 1996 and is buried alongside her husband. They had been married for 59 years.

The Akwesasne, Six Nations Indian Museum in Ourchiota, New York sent a resolution proclaiming:

Whereas, Sakoiteau. Our Creator, the Great Spirit, has seen fit to take from this life our esteemed Brother, Friend and fellow worker among our people, Ta-io-wai-ron-ha-gai (Dr. William B. Newell), and whereas his passing is indeed an inestimable loss to all of us as a race, and we realize thereby that another of our great who has many, many times brought honor, respect and good to his Indian People. . .has taken the Sunset Trail. His passing is a great loss to Indian America and especially to his Iroquois People, the Six Nations. His life, his great wisdom, his friendship, his courage and his defense of Indian truth will be a Light, a beacon that others may follow. One who was always ready to stand in the front line and help his people.

Be it therefore resolved: that we the members of the Akwesasne Mohawk Six Nations Indian Museum, extend our sincere sympathy to the sorrowing bereaved nearest him and his Kin, that we deplore their great loss and while they mourn their loss, they mourn the loss of us as a race, the Red Race of America.

Be it resolved that a copy of this resolution be presented to the Family of the deceased and a copy be placed on the wall of the Six Nations Indian Museum in his, Ta-io-wai-ron-ha-gai's honor.

Summary of Life Events

Thus, my father's life unfolded into a full 88 years of devotion to the American Indians and their contributions to civilization. He lectured across the nation to hundreds of institutions of higher learning, civic organizations, schools and churches. He had a long career in teaching and counseling once he educated himself from age 21, working his way through college, raising a family of five children through the Great Depression and two World Wars.

He worked from theater film projectionist at 16 years of age to owner of the American Indian Museum of Arts and Science at age 50. He graduated from Syracuse University in 1924 and then from the University of Pennsylvania in 1934. He eventually became a well-respected sociology, and anthropology professor at the University of Connecticut and the University of Florida.

In the four years from 1924 -1928, father served humanity as a missionary among the Seneca Indians on the Cattaraugus Reservation in New York. He is credited with saving the lives of many residents who were ill with tuberculosis and other diseases like diabetes by transporting them to hospitals for treatment and securing public health clinics on the reservation.

William B. Newell was instrumental in the formation of many organizations in his lifetime to include Caughnawaga Historical Society of Canada, Six Nations Society, Museum of Science and Natural History of Tampa, Big Soldier Playground of Mayetta, Kansas, and the Society of Neighborhood Indians of Philadelphia.

He participated in journalism from the time he was a sports reporter for the Syracuse Herald during his undergraduate college days to later years as sponsor of the

Brandon High School's newspaper, The Eagle's Eye. The Eagle's Eye won five honorary awards as an outstanding school publication receiving a National First Place award by the Columbia Scholastic Press in 1955.

Besides his missionary work he became an ordained minister for the Presbyterian Church in 1939, having attended Delany Divinity School in the years he ministered to the Seneca Indians in 1924 – 1928. He then served as a visiting pastor on Long Island, and ministered to the Shinnecock Indians who lived near the town of South Hampton.

At one time he was an ethnologist at Brooklyn Museum(1938); gave lectures for Pratt Art Institute for ten years on American Indian Art and Life; operated Rolling Thunder's Gift Shop and Tea Room (1927-1932); was Chief Clerk with the War Department at Montauk Point, N.Y.(1940-43); Fire Chief at Fort H.G. Wright Army Post on Fisher's Island(1943-46); and public school teacher at Mango Elementary School, and Brandon High School, Hillsborough County, Tampa, Florida (1949-1961). He was a long time 32nd degree Mason.

He had a listing in Who's Who in America in 1950-52, 1964-65; included in the American Academy of Political and Social Sciences; American Association of University Professors; American Anthropological Association; American Association of Museums; Veteran of the Foreign Wars; Phi Delta Kappa, honorary professional fraternity; and many others too numerous to list.

His publications include The Quipa, The Six Nations periodicals, the 36th Annual Archeological Report for Provincial Museum of Toronto, "Crime and Justice Among the Iroquois Nations" (1965), and a pamphlet

"Contributions of the American Indian to Modern Civilization" (1939).

This latter publication can be found in the appendix. It demonstrates Ta-io-wai-ron-ha-gai's (William B. Newell) most important message still viable to all of us today.

Joyce Kassanonkwas Newell Sundheim

October 2018

Appendix I: Contributions of the American Indian to Modern Civilization by William B. Newell, 1939 (excerpts)

Social psychologists and anthropologists claim that when two individuals or groups of people associate together for any length of time there is a tendency on the part of these individuals or groups to become alike in their dispositions, personalities, and in their ways of living and doing things. In other words, an exchange of culture takes place between these individuals or groups, which has a tendency to create an entirely new and different culture complex and at the same time make them more evenly balanced culturally. For a simple illustration of this phenomenon, we might point out that married people after several years of constant companionship tend to become alike in many of their habits, actions, and ways of doing things. This same theory applies to larger groups of people who have distinctly different cultural backgrounds.

A few scientists became intensely interested in the science of acculturation and selected the American Indian as a subject for study. These men were interested in learning to what extent the American Indian has been affected by contact with European peoples and to what extent he has become a "white man." In contrast, your writer has been studying the subject from the other way around and has sought to determine to what degree the European has become an "Indian," since there is unquestionably, an even exchange, more or less of cultural traits between the European people and the American Indian- since the advent of the white man to the New World some four or five hundred years ago. We often hear it said that the white man taught the Indian only evils and none of the white man's virtues. Perhaps the time will eventually come when we can honestly say that the American Indian "taught the white man only his virtues and no evils."

The first important process in our study is differentiating between what is Indian culture and what is European culture. It is simple enough to make a study of the socio cultural relations between two modern communities, such as Middletown and New York City and arrive at some basic conclusion regarding the cultural differences existing between these two communities. However conducting a similar research between two groups that lived some four or five hundred years ago and determine to what degree they affected each other involves a tremendous amount of research.

This paper in no way attempts to set forth the data involved in a comparative study of these cultures but merely brings to the attention of social psychologists and students of cultural exchange, or acculturation, the problem involved, and respectfully points out several interesting factors that must be considered in a study of this sort. Secondly, it is hoped that it may inspire some readers with the incentive to enlarge upon the thesis and give the world a true picture of American Indian Culture, and prove beyond doubt that what we call Americanism today is a combination of Indian and European cultures.

The American Indian today, after five hundred years of contact, retains a large percentage of his native culture even after struggling against strong forces which have sought to break down his culture and inculcate into his personality European cultural traits.

In spite of the concentrated efforts and close proximity of European peoples in their endeavor to force upon the American Indian their culture the result has been failure to a very large extent. This emphasizes the fact that today over half of the 6,000 Iroquois Indians living in the thickly populated State of New York, still retain their ancient religious concepts and beliefs.

One must take into consideration not only the effect of social contact with the American Indian in the exchange of cultures but also with the socio-economic aspect into which the European was thrown upon his arrival in the New World. Primitive economy was responsible to a high degree for a comparatively even exchange of cultures in this particular field.

Naturally, the speed of acculturation would depend entirely upon the degree of exposure to such Indian groups and their associated behavior. The degree of infiltration and incorporation would also have to be taken into account. Naturally those who came to the New World during the first 250 years would be more apt to have absorbed and inculcated Indian culture on their own personalities than those who came during the past two hundred years. We know that many Indians sociological and philosophical ideas were taken to Europe with the first contact made with the American Indian. But after the first 250 years sufficient exchange had taken –place to definitely establish new cultural traits which have given birth to new ideas heretofore unknown in the Old World.

The problem before us is to determine the affect of this exchange of culture upon European peoples and <u>not</u> upon the Indians. We want to determine conclusively, some of the outstanding contributions of the American Indian to modern social culture and civilization. . . .

Indian political theories as embraced in the League of the Iroquois are important and stand out in marked contrast to the European theory of "the divine right of kings," which flourished in Europe at the time of the discovery of America. The individual rights of man were recognized in America long before the Europeans awakened to this political philosophy. Ideas of freedom, liberty, and equality existed and were engraved in the hearts of the Indians when Europeans were "boiled or roasted" whenever they spoke out against the state or church. One of the outstanding differences between the European and the American Indian was the fact that in America the Indian was permitted freedom of thought while in Europe an individual's thinking was done for him by autocratic and dogmatic leaders.

It was from the Iroquois League that we first learned the meaning of true democratic ideals. It was here that we learned what freedom of speech, freedom of worship, equal representation, and constitutional government really meant. It was here that real statesmen served their constituents faithfully, without any other pay than the honor, respect, and esteem of their people.

Governor Cadwallader Golden who wrote the first American History in 1727, some fifty years before the revolutionary war, tells us that these men "were elected on the basis of their merit, because of their honesty and integrity, and that they were usually the poorest men in the nation; never keeping anything for themselves, but distributing all annuities and monies equally among the people." It was in this first history that the early colonists were informed that here existed a "true democracy." Here are listed some customs which were a part of the everyday existence of Indians.

Dictators were unknown among the Iroquois. No man could tell another what he should do. Every man was allowed to decide for himself what he should do. Even the Sachems and "Chiefs" suggested but never commanded or insisted too strongly. To do such a thing would immediately lower them in the estimation of the people and cause their removal from office. "We Counsel Together" was a famous phrase of Iroquois and every man was allowed freedom of expression.

Government had a central seat where representatives of the several nations met to discuss state matters and where unanimous decisions only were rendered.

Humane: Indians were gentle and kind: (a) They never whipped their children but still retained the love and respect of their children all through life. They were unlike the Spartans who tied their boys to whipping posts each morning and lashed them to make them cruel and savage warriors. (b) They cared for their old people, and among the Iroquois an elderly person was never heard of who did not have a home and food to eat. (c) Father Pierre Biard, the first Jesuit priest to reach America in 1611 says that "if it had not been for the kindness and hospitality of the Indians they would have perished the first three winters they lived in America."(d) The Pilgrim Fathers were welcomed and cared and nursed back to health by the same Indians who had been pillaged and plundered by adventurous Europeans for over seventy-five years before the arrival of the Pilgrims. It was these same Indians who had lost their own sons, fathers and grandfathers to marauding kidnappers from Europe who then took their human cargo to Spain and sold them as slaves.

Quarreling: All the Jesuit writers inform us, was never seen in Indian homes, towns or communities. Even today, one hardly ever sees two Indians quarrel unless they may be intoxicated. It is significant that deadly weapons are never found on their persons. They do not carry guns, daggers or blackjacks. They are not cowards.

Bullies: are unknown among the Indians. There is no place in history where any Indian nation was the first to start a war between the white and the Indians. It is unknown for an Indian to take unfair advantage of an adversary. There is not a record of an Indian war that was not first announced to the enemy.

Among children the common school bully is unknown.

Character: Sir William Johnson, British Indian agent, after thirty-five years association with them stated "they are only beginning to deceive in their transactions with us." In another of his documents he stated that he has even tried to make an Indian steal but failed. Lying was punished by death.

Freedom of Women: Women received the honor and respect that no other people gave their women. There is not a single court record in the State of New York documenting an arrest of an Iroquois Indian for insulting or assaulting any woman. In all the lying, militaristic propaganda written about the Indians during the Revolutionary War, or any other war for the purpose of arousing hatred in the hearts of the people against the Indian, no single writer has dared say that the sanctity of womanhood was ever desecrated by an Indian warrior. . . The respect that Indians gave to all women is characteristic of the Iroquois Indians. Indian women enjoyed equal rights with men, and is some cases, were even considered superior to men. In some parts of the world, women are not even supposed to have souls.

Birth Control: was practiced among the Iroquois, and the family was no larger than three or four children.

Trial Marriage: The Jesuit priests inform us that trial marriage was practiced.

Health: Bathing has become more or less common now among white people, but when America was first discovered, Europeans did not bathe the body because it was considered a mortal sin to make the body beautiful by cleaning it. This accounts for the numerous skin diseases brought to America by Europeans. Measles, smallpox, chicken pox and all skin diseases were non-existent in America prior to that. . .we know that Indian villages had several Turkish baths. Some Indian tribes had a bath cult, where it was a part of their religion to bathe and keep clean. Sunlight and bathing have become the order of the day and exposing the body to sunlight and fresh air, like the Indian did is making the modern American healthy and strong. Hiking clubs and soldiers are now taught how to walk like the Indian.

Cruelty: Our American Indians learned how to be cruel from the Europeans. Burning at the stake was a European custom introduced to Indians by the Spanish, French and English. Joan of Arc was burned alive sixty-one years before Columbus discovered America. The Apache Indians had never heard of scalping until it was first introduced by our own soldiers back in 1881. When America was first discovered it was believed by Europeans that anyone who knew not Christ was an infidel and it was their duty to burn all infidels.

Equality: It is told by many explorers that no one Indian had more than his fellow man and that when one was hungry they were all hungry. They shared their food equally among their captives and with strangers.

Gambling: Indians loved to gamble but strange as it may seem, at the end of their game it was customary to return all winnings to the losers.

Brotherhood-of-Man: The Indians always called the white man "brother" in all of his dealings with him. He never called him "master, your majesty," or any other title which would indicate that he considered him a superior or a lesser being. Every man was trusted and deceit was never looked for in a fellow man. White people first coming to America were given a place to build their lodge but never under any circumstances did the Indian give or sell outright to him land which was supposed to be free to all human beings.

Not only did the American Indians teach us all of ideas of social democracy but also he contributed vastly to our economics.

The following list of food plants and economic contributions are only a few of the many that exist. There are hundreds of others not mentioned here. The fact to bear in mind is that these were known to the Indian, and used by the Indian long before the Europeans discovered America and eventually taken over by the white man.

Corn is a culture as well as every other economic product or plant taken up by the white man. When Indian corn was accepted it meant taking the whole culture; husking pins, corn cribs, husking bees, "barn dances." and the forty or fifty ways of preparing corn for eating.

The following are only a few such articles which involved hundreds of minor cultural traits:

Potatoes (among the Aymara Indians no less than 240 varieties were cultivated), Tomatoes, Pumpkins, Squashes, Lima Beans, Kidney Beans, Peppers, Coca(Cacao) Pineapples, Nispero, Barbadoes, Cherry,

Strawberries, Persimmons, Papaws, Guava, Oca, Cashew, Nut, Pacay, Jocote, Star Apples, Mate Tea, Alligator Pear, Sour Sop, Sweet Sop, Custard Apple, Cassava(first necessary to remove deadly prussic acid from plant before edible and the poison sometimes used as a preservative to prevent putrefaction of meat), Cucumber, Peanuts, Maple Sugar.

Then there is: Tobacco, Quinine (an important medicinal contribution), Casa Sagrade (most important laxative), Cocaine (important drug used extensively by Indians in Pre-Columbian days), Cotton (Indians wore the first cotton clothing in the world), Henequen (hemp), Rubber(Indians first invented rubber), Copal(an important varnish), Peruvian Balm, Sunflower, Parica(in South America only). (No intoxicating beverages or drugs were used in North America).

Flavors: vanilla, chocolate, pineapple, maple, strawberry.

Asceptics: The Indian was the first to use boiled water for cleansing and dressing wounds.

Trephining: An important surgical operation whereby a section of the skull bone is removed to relieve pressure on the brain; was frequently performed by the Indians of Peru.

Science: In the field of science the American Indians were clever. Zero was invented a thousand years before the Arabians came out with it in the Old World. The calendar system of the Maya Indians was far superior to our own system and much more accurate. The first people to develop the decimal system represented in the Quipu of the Peruvian were Indians (hundreds of years before white man).

Metallurgy: Indians worked with gold, silver, and bronze better than any of the ancient civilizations of the Old World, and the first to use and work Platinum.

Arts and Crafts: The famous textiles of the Peruvians have long been recognized by authorities as being the best the world has ever seen. Authorities claim that no race on earth made baskets as well as the Poma Indians of California.

Agriculture: Irrigation, fertilizers, crop rotation, and many other so called modern farming methods were practiced extensively by the Indians of the Southwest in the United States and in Peru.

Masonry: The stone walls of Cuzco are still a great mystery to us, not knowing how the stones were quarried and so well fitted together. Modern apartment buildings are much like the Pueblo buildings of the Hopi and Zuni Indians.

Chewing Gum

Shaking Hands is just a good old Indian custom in some places.

Appendix II: Message from William B. Newell

(Sent to the young people of the Akwesasne Mohawk Counselor Organization) by William B. Newell

"You have within you the thing that makes it possible to do all things. You can do good things or you can do bad things. In the long run it is the good things that count most. I have always been a hater of liquor and do not want to see my people lose their chance to enjoy the good in life by indulging in liquor for the bad things in life.

America, the United States of America, is said to be a mixture of accumulated cultures from the different peoples of the world. By a slow process if acculturation and assimilation over a period of one, two, three hundred years we have today a nation created out of this combined cultures of those who have come to our shores from different parts of the world.

In the final analysis of present day times, the Iroquois Peoples should feel proud of the part they have played in contributing to modern civilization their great and glorious cultural attributes. Outstanding, and above all, were their ideas of peace, brotherly love, and way of life. They knew how to live well with each other and especially with their children.

Iroquois peoples as well as Americans of all races and nationalities would do well to retain, preserve and emulate some of the ideologies and cultural traits of the

Ho-de-no-sau-ne."

William B. Newell

Chairman Sociology Department

University of Connecticut

New London, Connecticut

(1948)

Appendix III: What I Believe About Jesus Christ
By William B. Newell

(Ta-io-wah-ron-ha-gai) 1950

No one has ever asked me before to tell what I believe about Jesus Christ. The question embarrasses me to some extent it isn't often that you are asked to express your personal convictions to the general public on such an intimate question as your religious beliefs. As a matter of fact it is not an easy or simple question to answer and my replies, I fear, may seem contradictory. Furthermore I feel almost certain that my ideas and beliefs will not be in accord with the popular conception or perhaps I should say with the orthodox conception as formulated in the great church creeds and confessions. But since this is an intelligent question I am going to try my best to give an intelligent answer.

First of all, if there is one single concept that is generally accepted by all these individuals who profess themselves followers of Christ then I have never heard of it. Ever since I was a little boy I have listened to many followers of Christ and I have never been satisfied that any of them knew definitely what it was they believed about Jesus Christ. What I mean to say is that none of them seem to be completely in agreement with each other. There seems to be so many aspects and so many ways of looking at Christ that to accept one and not the others puts you in a different category and you become an outsider in the eyes of many groups.

My next great problem in trying to formulate a creed is that I feel compelled by circumstance to give four versions of my creed based on four life experiences; each has a different point of view about Christ. My life has been cast in four molds. The first mold covers that period from early childhood to the time I reached my twenty-first birthday. In this first period I could neither read nor write and was a non-Christian. The second casting of my life begins with my sudden realization that in order to get anywhere in this world one must learn to read and write. During this second casting I became a Christian, secured a college degree, served two years in France with the A.E.F, and for about seven years was a missionary to some native peoples on our Indian reservations. Then, the third of my life begins about the year 1933 when I decided to change my profession from that of a missionary to that of a college professor. I like to think of the third of my life as that of an anthropologist and teacher of history. The fourth and last period of my life begins with my becoming a teacher in the public school system of America. In order to make this change I selected Florida as ideal for climatic reasons and because the public school system of Florida in my opinion is the best in America.

It is my firm conviction that my thinking on Christ has been affected most seriously by my four life occupations. It is perhaps more appropriate then that I begin my dissertation with a statement on what I believe about Jesus Christ from the point of view of a public school teacher. It is almost a daily occurrence for a public school teacher to discuss some phase of democratic government and the democratic processes or concepts. When one discusses the democratic philosophy or any phase of democratic government the obviousness of similarity of the principles expressed in the teachings of Christ and our democratic way of life as expressed in the government of the United States, especially its social aspects, is inescapable.

It is assumed, of course, that the average teacher has some knowledge of Christian teachings and ethics, and the ideas that Christ brought into this world. A school teacher must have some definite idea about Christianity and our democratic form of government in order to be able to recognize the things each has in common. Children have the knack of asking the most unexpected questions about religious doctrine, and if you are a good teacher and the children like you they are going to look to you for an answer to their question; or at least a reasonable answer to their questions. A few people realize that tremendous responsibility of the public school teacher. They must, under nearly all circumstances, give the child a serious reply to a serious question. Giving logical and sensible answer to vital questions is dangerous and serious business. The slightest indifference or belittling of any question on the part of the teacher may leave in the mind of the child a feeling of doubt and uncertainty. These impressions have a tendency to stay with a child all through his or her life. The psychological effects may destroy the child's ability to accept right from wrong. Incidentally, the opportunity under each under such circumstances for the subversive person who has no God are dreadful to contemplate. Senator McCarthy is convinced that even among the professionals; legal, ministerial, professorial, and instructional subversive elements can and do exist.Under these circumstances, as a teacher, I am most sincerely believe that there can be no democratic form of government without using the Christian concept of ideas and ethics as basic guides to our instructional conduct. To formulate a better government, create a better society, in a better world, Christ and his teachings must be accepted, and inculcated in the hearts of all peoples.

I am firmly convinced that our leaders, political and otherwise, must except the teachings of Christ in their entirety, especially his doctrine of the brotherhood of man. As a teacher I believe that Christ did not intend that we have some 250 different versions of his Word. It is difficult for the teacher who belongs to one of these sects to mention religion to a group of children who may have dozens of different concepts of Christ taught them in their homes and in their Sunday schools. I believe that Christ was logical and did not intend that we have more than one general broad concept without controversial features. As a teacher I am forced to respect all faiths and do not ever set any one belief above another, but try to interpret Christian teachings on a broad intelligent perspective. If we are to survive as a democratic nation we must educate our children in the ways of Christ by our way of life and our actions in and out of the classroom. Society must be preserved at all costs and above all else. The teacher has first chance at making this realization come true.

What I believe about Jesus Christ as a minister of the gospel of Jesus Christ, and as a former missionary and teacher among native American aboriginees over a period of several years is about as unorthodox as anyone can imagine. My ideas will not coincide with the many and varied ideas that will be advanced by other ministers of the Christian faith. Many of their concepts will be confusing and unintelligible and impossible to understand or comprehend. In my simple way, and I like to think of myself as being most humble in this respect, I will try to give a clear simple and sensible logical explanation of my belief of Christ to which I adhere and to concepts which have always seemed to satisfy my religious needs.

My primary belief is that Christ had a mission in this world and that mission was to bring happiness, peace, comfort and contentment to all the peoples of this world and not just to a special few. I do not believe that good deeds performed in this world and in His name necessarily receive a reward in the next world, but rather I am inclined to believe that the reward comes in this life. I do not believe that Christ was a mystic or that he wanted us to live by magic words and phrases and other superstitious practices, beliefs or customs.

I believe that Christ was practical and human and had ideas of making this world a better place in which to live rather than improving and preparing candidates for heaven and a life in the next world. I believe that too many preachers are using Christianity for selfish purposes and self-aggrandizement rather than for the benefit of the people under them. They persuade the acceptance of some form of Christianity concocted by them and at complete variance to the true teachings of Christ. There is too much fraud, too much insincerity, too much stupidity coming out of the pulpits of numerous sects of our country.

I believe that Christ intended us to aid, comfort, and succor the poor, the weak, the unfortunate, the sick, and the ignorant and especially the young and the aged. If these Christian beliefs be socialistic, if these Christ like ideas are the basis of promulgating a welfare state and are not true democratic ideals then why pretend to be Christian or even intimate that democracy is based on Christian ideals and ethics. One might ask why be democratic? But, what else can we be?

These then are my concepts of Christ and Christianity and the ones I most sincerely believe in. Some years ago when I was a missionary I well recall the action of the Board of Missions at the end of my first year, reprimanding me for my crusader tactics. During that first year I carried over 70 men women and children, mostly children, to the county tuberculosis sanitarium. The Board of Missions informed me that I was not supposed to do that kind of work and then henceforth I should let the appropriate organizations care for these people. (The trouble was they never did) While I was re-strained from giving aid to the sick and unfortunate people who were dying from tuberculosis I still felt that it was my duty, my Christian duty, and something that Christ, would've done above all things. In other words I believe that Christ was a social worker and sought improved conditions in our social life.

As a student and professor of anthropology over a period of 30 years my ideas and beliefs about Christ should be interesting. Religious development from the earliest time begins with a concept of a spirit world or a world of spirits. Everything from inanimate objects to animals, plants, and humans were or could be involved in this world of spirits and usually were. From this early theory of a spirit world down through the ancient days of the Egyptians, the Babylonians and the early Hebrew superstitious fears filled the hearts of men. Yes, we may go so far as to say that up until about 100 years ago hellfire and torment of threats of punishment after death or the thought of prospective rewards in the next world filled the hearts of men. Good deeds and indulgences were performed in order to seek after death "social security." It was even believed that sackcloth and ashes, suffering, self-inflicted bodily punishment, torture and other forms of mistreatment, even to the extent of starving ones-self in this world would result in future rewards in the next world.

Ignorance has been the greatest drawback to developing a true Christian way of life, and that of social justice and true democracy. In addition to ignorance we must also consider greed and selfishness the second greatest drawback to true democracy. Christ is the most practical deity this world has ever known. Superstition is not a necessity to believing. Every day we come a little bit nearer to realizing that democracy and Christianity are one and the same thing.

The anthropologist has learned that all mankind must have some deity even to our most intellectual men and women. The concept of a "Great Spirit" or one God is not specifically an early Hebrew concept. In all probability the American Indian long believed in one "Master of Life" or the "Great Spirit" long before the early Hebrews gave up their polytheistic beliefs and adopted one God, Jehovah. Primitive people all had their gods and representatives of their gods. The great religious of mankind today still have their gods and representatives of their deities. The Muslims have their Mohamed, the Christians their Jesus. It is most fortunate that the Christians have a God who's representative teaches us the universal brotherhood of man and the ideals involved in this doctrine. It is the most practical and the most scientific religion in the world today. It is my opinion the salvation of the world is through Jesus Christ.

If I were to say what Christ means to me as an American Indian only, then I am afraid that what I believe about Him would not be very flattering. First, I fear that my Indian concept would be that He is not taken too seriously by his followers since most people who deal with Indians as missionaries, teachers, and government agents on Indian reservations - do not usually practice the Christian tenants which they preach. In other words the American Indian has been and still is very badly treated by those who deal with him, so much so,that as an Indian I do not believe that Jesus Christ inspires sufficient sincerity and brotherly love in his followers. There is a weakness someplace along the line.

As an Indian I must admit that the ideas advanced by Christ for way of life are sound and well taken because they are identical with those practiced by the early Iroquois tribes in dealing with their fellow man. There **was** brotherly love. There **was** neighborliness and hospitality. There **was** charity. There **was** equality among individuals and a way of life based on democratic principles which was an inspiration to those who followed the Iroquoian philosophy of life, and especially to the followers of democratic Iroquoian government; and there **was** worship of the "Great Spirit" or God among those people.

The only difference between the Indian's religion and the Christian's religion is that the Indian **practiced** his religious beliefs whereas the Christians merely believed in them.

Appendix IV: North American Indian Traveling College Definitions

1. MOHAWK- Kanienkehake-Onkwehonwe

    We are called Mohawk, but this word is not our language. Our name Kanienkehake means "People of the Flint," because in our original homelands we had an abundance of flint and were known as the ones who made arrowheads and other tools. Onkwehonwe is a name we give all native people. It means "the original or real people."

2. THE PEACEMAKER

    This man came to different nations bringing the ideas of PEACE and UNITY. The idea is that with logical minds we, can sit and discuss things instead of resorting to violence.

3. CLAN

    A large family that is related matrilineal to each other. Among the Mohawk People there are 3 primary clans; the BEAR, WOLF, and TURTLE. There are also other clans among the Mohawks but smaller; the DEER and SNIPE.

4. CLAN MOTHERS

    The leaders of our families are women who hold the power to put the chiefs into office.

5. GREAT LAW of PEACE

    This is the epic story of how the Peacemaker came to the Haudenousaunee People. Within this story are laws, lessons, songs, wampum and the ways we are to guide our lives. This is an oral tradition that takes approximately ten days to recite.

6. WAMPUM

A shell bead made from the quahog shell, found along the shoreline. This bead was used in trade and during important ceremonies. These beads became valuable because of the difficulty in producing them. The wampum bead carries on a long spiritual tradition among our people. It is greater than the standard definition of "Indian Money." It was an important tool for communicating to the creator as well as to each other. It was used when forming treaties.

7. SONGS and DANCES

Standing Quiver is a type of STOMP dance – usually the first dance at an Iroquois social.

Then there are the following named dances: Friendship Dance , a partner dance, Old Moccasin Dance shows off fancy footwork, Robin Dance, a flat footed side-step dance, Stick Dance, Shake The Bush Dance, Round Dance, Women's Dance, Alligator Dance, Passenger Pigeon Dance, Rabbit Dance, Duck Dance, and Unity Stomp Dance. Many of these that are performed at an event, include singing and the use of drums.

Notes

1. " Texas Lillie," Shooting Star of the Lone Star State by Rolling Thunder, Louis B. Newell, 1989
2. NE-DO-BA, website, a non-profit 501(c)(3) public charity mc State of Maine, Friends Sharing History
3. The Montreal Herald, February 17, 1919
4. The Montreal Star, February 17, 1919
5. Photo of William Newell w/ Edison Movie Projector by Alexander Menire, Sept 21, 1912- Nov.16, 1914
6. Gervais Macomber and His 26 Children in Kahnawake by John Masiewicz, 2016, 2nd.Edition.
7. Crime and Justice Among the Iroquois Nations by William B. Newell(Ta-Io-Wah-Rob-Ha-Gai(Mohawk Band #15794), written 1934, pub. 1964
8. Caughnawaga Historical Society, 1965, Montreal, Canada
9. The Indian Life, Quarterly, 1978
10. The Montreal Star, June 15, 1963
11. The Montreal Star, October 10, 1962
12. The Tampa Tribune-Times, October 24,1976
13. St. Petersburg Times, November 4, 1976
14. Tampa Herald-Tribune, March 1, 1977
15. The Tampa Tribune, November 26, 1976
16. Bangor Daily News, December 10-11, 1977
17. MonchengladBacher Stadtpost, Germany, April 7, 1964
18. The Tampa Tribune, February 12, 1976

19. The National Police Gazette: New York, July 26, 1890
20. Indians of Today, Marion E. Gridley, Chicago, 1947
21. Kahnawake, by Johnny Beauvais, 1985
22. The Six Nations, Gowanda News Print, N.Y., Feb. And Oct. 1927, Apr. and July 1928, April 1929
23. Contributions of the American Indian to Modern Civilization by William B. Newell, 1939 (excerpts)
24. NewEnglandHistoricalSociety.com
25. Algonquians of the East Coast, Time-Life Books, 1995
26. "The Fire That Never Dies," Harvey Arden, National Geographic, September, 1987

Joyce Kassanonkwas Newell Sundheim

jsundheim@gmail.com

2018

Made in the USA
San Bernardino, CA
24 November 2018